D0461470

CALGARY PUBLIC LIBRARY

JUL - 2010

LIVING FOR THE WEEKDAY

*What Every Employee and Boss Needs
to Know about Enjoying Work and Life*

CLINT SWINDALL

WILEY

John Wiley & Sons, Inc.

Copyright © 2010 by Clint Swindall. All rights reserved.

Published by John Wiley & Sons, Inc., Hoboken, New Jersey.

Published simultaneously in Canada.

No part of this publication may be reproduced, stored in a retrieval system, or transmitted in any form or by any means, electronic, mechanical, photocopying, recording, scanning, or otherwise, except as permitted under Section 107 or 108 of the 1976 United States Copyright Act, without either the prior written permission of the Publisher, or authorization through payment of the appropriate per-copy fee to the Copyright Clearance Center, Inc., 222 Rosewood Drive, Danvers, MA 01923, (978) 750-8400, fax (978) 646-8600, or on the web at www.copyright.com. Requests to the Publisher for permission should be addressed to the Permissions Department, John Wiley & Sons, Inc., 111 River Street, Hoboken, NJ 07030, (201) 748-6011, fax (201) 748-6008, or online at http://www.wiley.com/go/permissions.

Limit of Liability/Disclaimer of Warranty: While the publisher and author have used their best efforts in preparing this book, they make no representations or warranties with respect to the accuracy or completeness of the contents of this book and specifically disclaim any implied warranties of merchantability or fitness for a particular purpose. No warranty may be created or extended by sales representatives or written sales materials. The advice and strategies contained herein may not be suitable for your situation. You should consult with a professional where appropriate. Neither the publisher nor author shall be liable for any loss of profit or any other commercial damages, including but not limited to special, incidental, consequential, or other damages.

For general information on our other products and services or for technical support, please contact our Customer Care Department within the United States at (800) 762-2974, outside the United States at (317) 572-3993 or fax (317) 572-4002.

Wiley also publishes its books in a variety of electronic formats. Some content that appears in print may not be available in electronic books. For more information about Wiley products, visit our web site at www.wiley.com.

Library of Congress Cataloging-in-Publication Data:

Swindall, Clint, 1967–

   Living for the weekday : what every employee and boss needs to know about enjoying work and life / by Clint Swindall.

      p. cm.

   ISBN 978-0-470-59940-2 (acid-free paper)

   1. Quality of work life.   2. Work environment.   3. Management—Employee participation.   4. Corporate culture.   I. Title.

   HD6955.S974 2010

   658.3′14—dc22   2010012329

Printed in the United States of America

10 9 8 7 6 5 4 3 2 1

*To my good friend and mentor Earl Moseley,
whose enthusiasm for life and love for God
set the example for living for the weekday.
(1962–2010)*

CONTENTS

Career → relationship → health, finance) spirituality.

Introduction

Seven days in a week. It's one of the few things we all have in common. From there, we all head in different directions regarding how we see—and spend—those seven days.

Some people devour them. They wring every ounce out of each day, enjoying every minute as though it just may be their last. Whether they're working or playing doesn't matter. They're just happy to be alive, and they're the exception to the rule.

Most everyone else—the clear majority of the people you encounter each day—make up the rule. They split their seven days into two categories: work and home. Work is the necessary evil required to survive and pay the bills, and home (or any place other than work) is the place they long to be.

Some people question how we ever got to the point of allocating five days to business and two days for ourselves. Some researchers identify the ancient Sabbath as the origin of the current so-called weekend, with the day before Sunday needed at home to make preparations for a proper observance of the Sabbath the next day. Others believe it was an attempt by labor unions to accommodate Jewish workers who took Saturday instead of Sunday as their Sabbath. And, according to a few of my friends, Saturday is required to get everything together to watch sports on Sunday.

Regardless of how we got here, the precedent is set. Most full-time jobs require five days of work during the week, with two days off for the weekend. And although this makes work a significant part of life, most people don't like to work. They don't like their job. They don't like their boss. They don't like their colleagues. As a result, most people don't want to be there.

Numerous studies support it. According to the Gallup Organization, three out of four people are 3/4 at some level of disengagement. One out of four is productive and wants to be at work, and the rest dominate the workplace with their waiting. They're waiting for the weekend. They're waiting for vacation. They're waiting for Friday. They're waiting for a boss to make them happy. They're waiting for a promotion. And every single week, they're living for the weekend.

It doesn't take a mathematician to figure out the numbers are against those who live for the weekend. With seven days in a week, disengaged employees spend five days staring at a clock in hopes the two days at the end of the week can bring them enough joy to sustain them until the next weekend.

I have spent many years of my life addressing the challenge of employee disengagement. In my first book, *Engaged Leadership*, I addressed the leader's responsibility to create a culture where employees want to work. Managers certainly have a motive to create this type of culture, and with the proper focus and support they can do it. But the reality is it's not their *only* focus, and some will be better at it than others. In order for a culture of engagement to truly develop, employees have a responsibility to show up with a certain level of personal engagement. Whether we like it or not, employee engagement is a two-way road.

Some people question why they should do anything to contribute to a culture of engagement in their professional life. Simply put, our work consumes too much of our time *not* to find ways to become more engaged. We can sit around and wait for the perfect job to come along. We can sit around and wait for the perfect boss to come along. Or we can do the best with what we have.

Some employers are taking risks and trying to alter the "five days of business, two days of pleasure" model. They've lengthened four days of the workweek and provided for three-day weekends. Some are using technology to allow more flexibility regarding when work is performed. But for many others in the workplace today, the "five days of business, two days of pleasure" model isn't changing any time soon.

So, what can we do about that? We can change how we view our professional life and personal life coming together. Instead of breaking our seven days into *work* and *home*, we can examine how the following five aspects must all weave together: *career, relationships, health, finances,* and *spirituality.* Each of these is important because they affect each other.

Consider this. I can't focus on my career—and be engaged at work—if I don't focus on my physical and emotional health. It is not possible to be unhealthy at home while being healthy at work. When I don't feel good, I usually don't want to go to work—and if I do, I'm probably not very productive. I can't focus on my career—and be engaged at work—if I'm doing a poor job of managing my finances and I'm unsure whether I can pay my bills. I can't focus on my career—and be engaged at work—if I'm struggling with a significant relationship at home or with a boss or colleague at the office. It is not possible to separate the emotions required to deal with these relationship challenges from our personal and professional life. Ultimately, it all ties together.

We benefit personally when we find a way to weave together these five aspects of our life, and our bosses benefit as well. You see, the leader can do everything outlined in *Engaged Leadership* and yet not create an engaged culture if the employees aren't doing their part. For instance, the leader can ensure an employee understands clearly the role he or she plays in an organization, but it won't matter if the employee isn't "there" because of a poor relationship with his or her spouse. The leader can create incredible reward systems to recognize superior performance, but it won't matter if employees aren't "there" because they are trying to figure out how to pay the bills because they have done a lousy job managing personal finances. Ultimately, it all ties together.

By understanding what makes us effective at each of the five preceding aspects, we can understand our responsibility to become personally engaged in life, which will eventually lead to being engaged at work. I could argue that we owe it to an employer to be more engaged at work, but in reality, we owe it to ourselves. Employee disengagement is a lose-lose situation: Our employers lose because they don't get the best we have to offer, and we lose because we waste the time we spend at work. We owe it to ourselves not to be like those people who drag themselves through the week in search of the weekend. We owe it to ourselves to start living for the weekday.

Finally, this book is for you, the employee. Don't love your job for your boss. Love your job for yourself. Your boss will ultimately benefit by gaining a more engaged employee, but it is okay if your focus is on yourself. After all, it's your life.

Are you ready? Are you ready to start living a life that will allow you to look forward to Monday as much as you look forward to Friday? It is my hope you are, and that you read this book with an unusual focus on the simplicity of making your life more enjoyable and, in turn, helping to build a culture of employee engagement. If you are, then settle in for a lesson about how to make it happen.

THE FORMAT

A great deal of thought went into the format of my first book, *Engaged Leadership*. We considered the many benefits of traditional how-to books, and compared them to the success of business fables. A combination of the two was chosen.

As a professional speaker, I tell stories. They include people, something to which we can all relate. I tell stories in my speeches because I see the light come on for many people when they learn a lesson through a story and instantly apply it to their own situation.

As I've traveled around speaking about *Engaged Leadership*, perhaps the most common comment I've received is related to the format of the book: "The book was so easy to read and apply. I learned the lesson in the fable, and got the tools I needed in the how-to portion at the end." Based on these types of comments, we will follow that same format in this book.

Those of you who learn through stories will learn the lessons of *Living for the Weekday* through a business fable. Those who prefer the how-to format will find a portion of this book was written just for you. In the end, it will all come together.

The value of this book to any reader comes down to one simple word: *application*. Whether you derive value from the fable, from the how-to portion, or from a combination of the two, it is my hope you take what you've learned in *Living for the Weekday* and make it a part of your life.

Enjoy your weekday like your weekend.
Work 7 days a week ., always put your thinking to

Don't ~~throw~~ your job b/c of your boss,
♡ your job b/c of you. for yourself

The Fable

The story is about Miles Freeman, a longtime Halifax employee struggling with the disengagement of everyone around him in a new office. As he watches the leadership team work to build a culture of employee engagement, he is perplexed by the people he works with who can't—or won't—find a way to enjoy their jobs as they wander through their personal issues. He collides with fellow employees while encouraging them to find their own satisfaction and ultimately contribute to a culture of engagement. But with the help of some insightful training on life balance, a little structure is brought to this idea of job satisfaction. What Miles thought was just attitude turns out to be much more.

Miles Freeman could never understand why so many people were unhappy at work. Throughout his entire career, he achieved a level of job satisfaction that most people didn't seem to experience. Regardless of the work he did, Miles found a way to enjoy his job.

It wasn't that Miles was smarter than everyone around him. He had completed high school and a few years of college, so he wasn't more educated than his coworkers. At 41 years old, he had spent a few decades in the working world, but so had most of the people around him. Sure, he was good at his job. In fact, he was one of the best. But his competence isn't what made him happy at work. The reason for his job satisfaction was simple. He had done the math. He knew he spent many more waking hours at work than he did with his family, and since he had to work, he refused to leave his happiness up to someone else.

You see, Miles had a clear understanding that job satisfaction was going to come from one of two places. One, he would have a job that was so great he would bounce out of bed every day ready to give his all. And yes, he had experienced a few of those jobs over the past two decades. Or two, he would take responsibility for his own happiness. He refused to sit around and wait for someone else to make him happy. He didn't wait for a boss to motivate him. If he was unhappy, he knew he had no one to blame but himself.

Since he always took his job satisfaction into his own hands, it wasn't a big surprise when he requested a transfer from his old job. Miles wasn't happy with his boss, and he knew he had to make a choice. He could choose to show up at work every day and join the ranks of the disengaged employees who filled the hallways of his department, or he could choose to make a change. It was time for a change.

THE CHANGE

Miles chose early in his career to work for a large, growing company. Despite the challenges in the economy, the company was doing well, and there were plenty of opportunities to grow and many places to work. He had just celebrated his twentieth year with Halifax, a large call center company with offices in central Texas. Although the corporate headquarters were located in New Jersey, the company had offices all over the country. A new call center had opened two years earlier just outside of Austin, and the company was looking for call center representatives to transfer to the new location. Miles thought this just might be the change he needed.

Miles had been a call center rep his entire career with Halifax, so the change was more about geography than anything else. He knew the job well, so he was confident he could step in and start doing the job immediately. The only difference would be the location and the people. He was moving from one of the best teams in the Dallas call center, and he was anxious to meet his new coworkers. Miles Freeman had no idea what he was about to experience.

A NEW START

Miles was told to report to work at 9:00 AM on that cold Monday morning in January and to ask for Jill Ramos, one of the managers of the call center. Since he would have the same duties as in his previous job, he didn't need training before he could start. However, since it was a new office, he didn't want to be late, so he arrived just after 8:00 AM. The HR manager had e-mailed him the code to the door in order to get in the building, so he was able to head right inside.

As Miles approached the entrance to the call center, the door flew open. He stood to the side as a group of employees walked out and went around the corner. Although each person in the group noticed him standing there, no one greeted him or asked whether he needed help. As he turned to walk through the door, he was greeted by a well-dressed, attractive lady on the other side.

"Can I help you with something?" she asked.

"Yes, I'm looking for Jill Ramos," Miles answered. "I've been transferred from the Dallas call center, and I was told to ask for Jill. My name is Miles Freeman."

"Well, welcome to the office, Mr. Freeman. You're early. That doesn't happen around here very often. I'm Jill."

"I was afraid I might get lost, so I decided to give myself plenty of time," Miles responded as he closed the door behind him. "Besides, I figured my new boss would want to spend some time with me before I started working."

"I'd be happy to introduce you to your new boss, but he's not here yet. He's starting tomorrow. He's some new kid out of college. The HR manager asked me to get you started today, but I'm late for an 8:00 AM meeting. My office is right over there. I'll see you there at 9:00 AM. In the meantime, you can hang out in the break room. Go back through that door and turn to your left. I'm sure you'll find a way to pass the time."

HURRY UP AND WAIT

Miles assumed Halifax had hired the same team to design all the break rooms for the company. After 20 years and many different offices, they all looked the same, even this relatively new office. He stood at the doorway and noticed six tables in the room. The group of employees that had nearly knocked him down getting out of the office sat at a table in the corner. A few in the group looked his way, but none said hello. A television hanging on the wall was playing a rerun of *The Golden Girls*. He scanned the rest of the room and noticed an employee with bright red hair sitting alone at a table reading a Tom Clancy novel. He walked over and sat down with her.

"Hi, my name is Miles Freeman," he said with a smile and an extended hand. "I'm new to the office. I just transferred from Dallas and today is my first day."

"My name is Deanna Curtis," she said as she closed her book and shook his hand. "It's nice to meet you. I just started working here myself—

November, I think. How long have you been with Halifax?"

"I just celebrated my twentieth anniversary," Miles replied with a little too much excitement. "I'm guessing you were just a child when I started with the company."

"Pretty much," Deanna answered dryly. "Why the transfer?"

"It was time for a change. It was a great office, and I liked most of the people. But quite frankly, I didn't like my boss."

"That happens," Deanna replied. "I didn't care much for my last boss. She left not long after I got here. I don't think she could handle the pressure. Now we're getting some new guy."

"We must be on the same team. I was just told my boss will be some new guy. He starts tomorrow, straight out of college."

"That must be the one," Deanna replied as she stood to return to work. "Good luck. I guess I'll be seeing you around. I've got to get to work. It's the start of another long week."

As Deanna started to walk away, Miles asked, "How do you know it's going to be a long week? It's just getting started."

"It's Monday, that's how I know. We're a long way to the weekend."

With some time to kill before his 9:00 AM meeting, Miles helped himself to some coffee and a few chuckles from *The Golden Girls*. Every time he laughed out loud, he got strange looks from the corner table. Who would laugh out loud at reruns of *The Golden Girls*? Apparently, Miles Freeman would.

LIGHT DUTY

It was an easy first day. Most employees had to spend the entire day in orientation and training. Since Miles had done this job for years, he certainly didn't need training, and the equipment was all the same.

Jill was in her cubicle when Miles walked in at 9:00 AM sharp. "I just need you to sign a few papers for me, Miles. We have you scheduled for a 9:30 shift this morning. I think you'll find everything is pretty much the same as in the Dallas call center."

Miles signed the transfer documents as Jill pushed them across the desk. "How long have you been a manager here?"

"Two years. I was promoted when we opened this office."

"Oh, so you were a call center rep before that," Miles said, more as a statement than a question.

"Yep. My entire career."

Miles would later learn that Jill had been one of the best call center reps in the Austin office and that she had been promoted for her performance. "Do you like it?"

"It's certainly different than working shifts as a call center rep. These past two months have been the hardest. Lots of changes with our new boss. By the way, there are 100 call center reps in the office and only four managers, so you'll be one of 25 employees on your team."

"Pretty much the same as before," Miles smiled, and then went straight to a computer station to get settled in for his shift.

HIGHLIGHT OF THE DAY

The best part of the day for Miles was getting to spend some time with the lady who ran the call center, Hannah Jaxson. As he was preparing to leave the call center in Dallas, Miles had a conversation with his boss about the new office. His boss had spoken very highly of Hannah, and said the company was expecting big things from this short, dark-haired dynamo. Although the call center was nearly two years old, she had taken over only about two months earlier, and she'd asked to meet with Miles at the end of his first day.

"You left one of the best call centers in the state," Hannah said as they sat down in her office. "Tell me why you left."

"I didn't like my boss," Miles responded plainly. "For years I loved working in that office. The culture was great. But when I got my new boss, we never hit it off."

Hannah nodded as if she'd experienced the same. "I've often heard that people don't leave companies, they leave bosses. I guess that was true for you."

"I guess so. I'm just fortunate enough to work for a large company so I could leave an office and not a company. So, what have I gotten myself into by transferring to this office?"

Hannah paused for a second as she considered her response. "I'm still trying to figure that out myself, since I've been here only two months. The culture is a work in progress. The office is driven by results, so there is certainly a healthy competitive environment. However, I'm not sure it's made much of a difference to some people. In fact, the team you're joining is in last place in every area we measure and has been for years."

Miles laughed out loud. "Great. Any idea how to fix that little problem?"

"Again, it's all a work in progress, but I think it's more about culture than ability. I'm hoping to get some help from the person who will be your boss. Maybe he can provide a little spark and get people excited about coming to work."

"I was told I was being assigned to the new guy," Miles replied. "What's his story?"

"His name is Seth Owen. He's a young management recruit. He'll probably be in this office for a year or so, but I'm hoping he can help develop the culture. I met with him a few weeks ago, and I think he has some potential."

"I've had a lot of bosses during my 20 years with Halifax," Miles replied. "Some have been younger, and some have been older. Some have been great, and some have made me wonder how they ever got promoted. I'm looking forward to working with him. Maybe some of the Dallas call center can rub off here."

Time would tell.

THE NEW GUY

Miles arrived early on his second day as well. He sat by himself in the break room drinking coffee and waiting for his shift to start. Everyone at the tables around him was talking about the "new guy" starting that day. Many of them had seen Seth Owen on his visit to the office a few weeks back, but now they were finally about to meet him.

Miles had settled in to start his shift at a computer station by the entrance to the call center when he saw Hannah running toward the door. After the door opened, he heard Hannah say, "Welcome. I saw you at the front door on the security monitor and realized I forgot to give you the code. Sorry about that. We'll get it taken care of today. Let me show you to your cubicle."

Miles thought to himself, "At least they gave me the code." He turned to see everyone peeking over the short cubicle walls of their computer stations to check out the new guy. He knew the curiosity level was always high with the arrival of a new boss, and this time was no different. After his own bad experience with a boss in Dallas, Miles was excited to be a part of welcoming a new manager. Excited, and admittedly a little curious.

DINNER CLUB

During his lunch break, Miles walked into the break room where the hot topic was still the arrival of Seth Owen. "Did you see him? He's a kid! I have children older than him," one employee grumbled as she joined her friends at a table. Miles just smiled as he walked over and sat down at a table by himself. A fellow worker walked over and introduced himself. "Hi, my name is Sydney Wells. I think we're on the same team."

"Hello, Sydney," Miles responded as he extended his hand, realizing this was the first person in a day and a half who had approached him. "My name is Miles."

"I hear you moved here from Dallas," Sydney continued as he pulled out a chair and sat down. "Have you gotten settled in yet?"

"Somewhat," Miles responded as he opened his lunch. "We bought a house a few miles from the office, and we've been getting settled the past couple weeks. It was hard to relax and enjoy the holidays when I knew I should be unpacking boxes."

"A group of us from our team gets together once a month for dinner at a restaurant down the street. You're certainly welcome to join us. We're meeting this Friday evening right after work. We call it the 'Dinner Club.' Not very creative, but none of us ever claimed to be all that creative!"

Miles smiled in agreement with the lack of creativity. "Other than eating, is there any purpose to this Dinner Club?"

"Not really. It's just an opportunity to get together. Sometimes we talk about the office, and sometimes we talk about what we're doing on the weekend. Mostly, we just celebrate the fact we made it through another month. It's just a small group, all from the same team. Some of us have been around awhile, so we can fill you in on working in this call center. We meet the first Friday of every month."

Miles hadn't done anything but unpack boxes since his arrival, so this was an easy decision. "Sounds good," Miles said. "I'm sure I'll need a break by Friday. Where should I meet you?"

"We meet at a place called La Cantina. It's about three blocks from the office. They have the best margaritas in town. We're meeting at 6:00 PM this Friday."

"I appreciate the offer," Miles said with a nod. "It will be nice to get out of the house. I'll meet you there."

WELCOME TO THE TEAM

Just as Miles sat down at a computer station after his lunch, he got a note from a shift coordinator instructing him to go to the conference room at 3:00 PM for a team meeting with his new boss. He was looking forward to meeting this new guy and finally getting to figure out who was on his team.

As he entered the conference room later that afternoon, Miles noticed there were only 10 chairs around the conference table and 25 employees filing into the room. He assumed there would be a mad dash for the chairs, but most people immediately stood along the back wall and didn't even move toward a chair. Miles saw Sydney take one of the chairs, and he quickly sat next to him. He noticed Deanna standing along the back wall, and observed most of his fellow team members were rather distant.

Seth was straight out of college, and he looked like a kid. What he lacked in age, he made up for with confidence. "Good afternoon. My name is Seth Owen, and as you know by now, I am your new manager. We don't have much time, and I want each of you to introduce yourself, so I'm not going to be saying much in this meeting. However, there are two things I want you to know. First, Hannah offered to divide this team to create four new teams in the office because, as a group, you have not performed well. I asked her not to do that."

Miles noticed the words Seth had chosen got the attention of a few of his fellow team members.

"Some of you may think I'm crazy for doing that," Seth continued, "particularly since I don't know any of you yet. But I don't need to know you individually to know you all have the potential to be the best in this office. I'm committed to helping make this team the best."

This guy is good, Miles thought to himself. Oddly confident for a guy who had never managed a team of employees, but good.

"Second, many of you in this room have been here a long time. Each of you has forgotten more about your job than I will ever learn. I have no plans to come in here and learn your jobs so I can tell you what you're doing wrong. My plan is to use my position as a manager to remove the road-blocks that keep you from being successful. I'll make you a deal. You do your job well, and I promise you I'll do mine well."

After Seth finished his little speech, everyone had an opportunity to introduce themselves. Sydney went first, and Miles followed so he could get it out of the way. Miles couldn't help but notice the tone in the room had changed significantly after Seth made his remarks. Seth had made a great first impression, and the curiosity had been satisfied. There was still a lot to be seen from this young man, but Miles knew it was a great first encounter.

As his fellow team members introduced themselves, they seemed to be more relaxed. There was some laughter, and a few people actually sat in the empty chairs at the conference table. Miles was happy to see the tone had changed. This was a good thing, but good things don't always last.

EVERYONE BACK TO WORK

Just as the last person had finished her introduction, a person Miles had yet to meet threw open the conference room door and said, "Your hour is up. Customer hold time is going through the roof because we're short 25 people. Everyone back to work."

Miles knew this person was either a shift coordinator or a manager. Shift coordinators were call center reps who wanted additional responsibilities but didn't want to be a manager. Her tone seemed to be a little harsh for a shift coordinator, so he assumed she must be a manager.

Miles also knew there were four managers in the office. He had met Jill on his first day, and now he had met Seth. As they walked out of the conference room, Miles looked at Sydney and whispered, "Who was that?"

"Carmen Fuentes," Sydney replied quietly with a frown. "She's one of the managers. Everyone hates working for her. As you could probably tell, she's not the nicest person in the world."

As he went back to work, Miles noticed his fellow team members seemed to drag themselves back to their computer stations. Seth had gotten everyone excited, and this Carmen lady seemed to have zapped them of their energy. No wonder everyone seems to be dragging themselves around the office, Miles thought to himself. He was just thankful he didn't have to work for her.

HUMP DAY

Although the call center operated on shifts, management scheduled shifts that worked with each person's personal schedule. Some reps preferred to work late at night, so they were almost always assigned evening shifts. Miles enjoyed spending evenings at home with his wife and kids, so he requested early shifts.

He was on duty at 7:45 AM the next morning when he noticed all the managers had gone into the conference room. Deanna drifted into the office right at 8:00 AM for her shift and sat at the computer station next to his.

"Good morning, Deanna. How's it going?"

Without even looking in his direction, Deanna replied with the same enthusiasm she shared earlier in the week. "Fine. It's hump day. We're halfway to the weekend."

Miles ignored her comment. "What's the story with the managers' meeting in the conference room this morning?"

"I don't know. I think it's some quarterly meeting Hannah has with them. I heard she's been introducing some sort of employee engagement program. Not sure what it's about."

Miles wasn't sure what it was about either, but he had encountered a few people in just a matter of days who could benefit from some sort of employee engagement program. In fact, he was sitting right next to one.

MEET THE FAMILY

At six feet four, Miles was nearly a foot taller than his wife Gabriela. She may have been smaller, but he considered her to be wiser when it came to most aspects of life.

"Well?" Gabriela asked as Miles walked into the doorway of the kitchen. "What do you think of this new job after a few days?"

Miles walked over and kissed her on her forehead. "Good. Nothing too exciting. Same job, different city. I've met the people on my team, and I've met my new boss. He's some new kid out of college. His name is Seth Owen."

"College boy, huh? There's nothing like trying to break in some new guy."

"I've had that opportunity a few times in my career," Miles laughed. "This one will have a good mentor, though. I got to spend some time with his boss, Hannah Jaxson. She runs the call center, and she seems pretty progressive. We'll see. How was your day?"

"Busy," Gabriela responded without looking up from the salad she was preparing. "I unpacked a few more boxes. Between getting the boys registered for school this week and the myriad of other after-school activities, I'm tired. But all is well. Dinner will be ready in a bit."

Miles adored Gabriela. They met in high school and started dating toward the end of their senior year. They married soon after, and spent most of their first decade of marriage traveling around and enjoying their youth. They both worked as call center reps at Halifax, and they had planned to have two children, three years apart. However, their plans changed with the arrival of twin boys, Benjamin and Michael, now 12 years old.

Both boys struggled with having to move and leave their friends behind. But, like most young boys, they were quickly making new friends. In fact, although Michael said his life was over after having to leave his "girlfriend" behind, he had already met a new girlfriend, and life was moving on. For the boys, making new friends was easy. Miles wondered if the same would be true for him, and he looked forward to getting to know his fellow team members.

At least Miles thought he looked forward to getting to know his fellow team members. If misery did indeed love company, these people would not want to meet Miles Freeman.

INTRODUCTION TO LA CANTINA

Miles hadn't enjoyed good Mexican food in a long time, so he was looking forward to meeting Sydney and the other employees for dinner at La Cantina that Friday evening. He went home before going to the restaurant, and now he was running a few minutes late.

As he walked into the restaurant, Miles looked around and saw Sydney and three other people sitting in the far corner to the left of the entrance. He recognized Deanna Curtis, the lady with the Tom Clancy novel he had met in the break room on his first morning.

"Hey, Sydney," Miles said as he approached the table.

"Hey, Miles. Everybody, this is Miles Freeman. He's new to our Halifax office." Miles scanned the group and received welcoming nods from everyone around the table.

Sydney pulled out a chair next to him and motioned for Miles to sit down. "We haven't ordered dinner yet. However, we just ordered a round of margaritas. It's their specialty. Would you like one?"

"I could be convinced," Miles responded with a smile as he walked over and sat down.

Sydney waved down the waitress and put in the extra order. "All right, everyone go around and introduce yourself. Tell Miles how long you've been around, and anything else you think he should know. Let's start with you, Mattie, and just go around the table."

"Hello, Miles. I'm Mattie Brown. I've been here a long time, nearly 20 years."

"Deanna Curtis . . . we met earlier in the week. Just been here a few months."

"I'm Larry Marcus. Been here too long."

"And, of course, I'm Sydney, the one who talked you into joining our little group for dinner. I've been around for 11 years."

"Well, thanks for including me," Miles said as he glanced around the table. "My wife and our two boys just moved here. I've been with Halifax for 20 years, most recently in the call center in Dallas. I'm just glad to be here."

"We're glad you joined us," Sydney responded. "We've started meeting here once a month. Nothing formal or fancy—just a chance to get together outside the office. If you don't get a chance to talk with everyone at the office, you'll at least get a chance here if you decide to come back."

About that time, the waitress came around and took everyone's order. Miles went last so he could have some time to look at the menu. As he waited his turn, he thought about how nice it would be to spend time with a group outside of work.

MR. DOOM-AND-GLOOM

Once all the orders had been taken, Deanna and Mattie started a conversation with Sydney. Miles used the opportunity to strike up a conversation with Larry.

"Were you at the team meeting earlier this week?" Miles asked as he turned to Larry. "I don't remember seeing you."

"I was there," Larry responded dryly as he sipped his margarita. "I was standing along the wall . . . last one in the room and the first one to leave when it was over."

"I thought the meeting went well," Miles said enthusiastically. "What did you two think?"

Larry looked over the rim of his glasses as if he was annoyed by the enthusiasm Miles showed. "More of the same. I've been around here a long time. I've seen managers come and go. They're all excited at first, and think they'll change the world. Give him a few months and it all will change."

Miles was somewhat taken aback by Larry's response. "Wow. I thought it went well."

"I agree with you, Miles," Sydney interrupted as he turned to join the conversation. "I thought he did a good job of setting the tone. Larry tends to look at the negative side of everything. He's Mr. Doom-and-Gloom."

"It's just that I've been around a long time," Larry replied as he finished his margarita and motioned for the waitress to bring him another. "These managers all watch out for themselves. They all talk a good game, but they seldom do anything to make it better for the employees. It's just a bunch of the same rhetoric. In time, we'll run this guy off as well."

As Larry was talking, Miles noticed Hannah Jaxson walk in the door. She waved at them as she headed for a corner table on the opposite side of the restaurant.

"She seems pretty sharp," Miles stated as he nodded his head in her direction. "I had a chance to spend some time with her earlier this week."

"Time will tell," Larry replied. "I hear she's already started some employee engagement thing." He said the words *employee engagement* like they caused a bad taste in his mouth.

"Is that a terrible thing?"

"New manager, new program," Larry responded as he continued to peer over the rim of his glasses. "Seen it all before."

Miles grinned and shook his head as he considered Larry's disposition. "Is there anything you like about working in this call center, Larry?"

"Dinner Club at La Cantina," he replied with the first and only grin of the evening.

Miles wondered two things. One, why did Larry even wear glasses? He never saw him actually look through the lenses. And two, how could one person carry that much negativity and still get out of bed in the morning?

AN INVITATION TO LUNCH

Miles enjoyed his job as a call center rep. Some of his coworkers seemed to stare at the clock until it was time for lunch, while Miles often found it hard to believe that half the day had gone by. As he was walking into the break room for lunch on that Monday afternoon, Sydney and Mattie were walking out.

"Hey, we're going across the street for lunch," Sydney commented to Miles. "You want to join us?"

Miles paused for a second as he looked at his watch. "Can we be back in an hour?"

"Less than that," Mattie responded. "My shift starts in 45 minutes, so we have to be back."

"I'm in." And with that, they were off to lunch.

LUNCH WITH MATTIE BROWN

"Is this place always this busy?" Miles asked looking around at the full tables.

"Always," Sydney replied as they sat down in a booth. "It's very popular with the employees from our call center. It's the closest restaurant to the office, and they're fast. You'll probably be eating here quite often."

"So, Mattie," Miles started, "we didn't get a chance to talk at La Cantina."

"Yeah, I saw you got stuck talking to Larry," Mattie replied with a grin. "Not such a great intro to Dinner Club, huh?"

Miles wanted to make a comment about Larry, but he held back. "What a treat that was! How long have you been with Halifax?"

"Eighteen years."

"Wow. Just celebrated 20 years myself," Miles responded with a smile. "It's actually hard to believe. It seems the years have flown by."

Mattie thought about his comment for a moment. "Most of those years flew by for me, too. Actually, 16 of them flew by. I can't say the same for the past two."

"What happened in the past two years? Isn't that when they opened the new office?"

"Yep," Mattie answered, "and they changed the teams. I was on Aaron's team before, and all was good, but I got changed to Carmen's team. It all went downhill from there."

"First of all, who's Aaron? And second, what's up with this Carmen lady?" Miles asked with a frown. "I haven't heard anything good about her since I got here."

Sydney chimed in. "Aaron King is one of the four managers. Seth, Aaron, Jill, and Carmen. As for Carmen, she's just bitter. She came to this office thinking she would get promoted to Hannah's position. When that didn't happen, she just became bitter. Come to think of it, she was bitter long before that happened. She seems to think you have to beat people up to get them to work. As a result, no one wants to work for her."

"Exactly," Mattie replied emphatically. "She just makes life miserable for everyone around her. I did the bare minimum to get by. My whole week was a countdown to Friday. I just did everything I could to avoid her."

"That's somewhat hard to do when you work for her," Miles laughed.

"True. Fortunately, I don't work for her anymore. I requested a transfer to another team last year, and they moved me to this team."

"Maybe it will get better now," Miles replied.

"Maybe. Seth's only been here a week, and I was the first person he called into his office. He said he noticed I had the worst attendance record of anyone on our team, and he needed for me to improve."

"Was he mean about it?" Sydney asked.

"Not at all," she replied. "Oddly enough, the way he talked about it kind of inspired me to do better."

"I can see why Carmen's employees are so miserable," Miles responded. "But what's up with everyone else? It seems most people are just dragging themselves around the office."

"Was it different in Dallas?" Sydney asked.

"We certainly had some miserable people, but nothing like here."

"I guess everyone is waiting to see what's going to happen with this new leadership," Mattie responded. "Maybe they think something will happen with Hannah and Seth to make it better."

Sydney added his thoughts. "Or maybe they're like most people and they're just counting down the days to the weekend. It's not like we're changing any lives in this job. We're just handling calls in a call center."

As they enjoyed their lunch, Miles wondered about Mattie. He liked her, and he felt sad she had such a bad experience that she just did the basics to get by. It was apparent to Miles she wanted to be engaged in her work, but it seemed she was waiting for someone else to motivate her. Miles knew she would need to provide her own motivation, or she would continue to be a wasted resource for the office. He hoped she'd find a way to rekindle her spirit now that Carmen was out of the picture. Little did he know, Carmen would never be out of the picture. People like Carmen never are.

QUIET TIME WITH GABRIELA

By the time Miles arrived home from the Dinner Club that previous Friday night, Gabriela had already headed off to bed, exhausted from a full week of running the boys around. He respected Gabriela's views, and had come to depend on her as a sounding board. He looked forward to sharing his observations with her over dinner.

"Where are the boys?" Miles asked as he walked into the kitchen.

Gabriela walked over for her "welcome home" hug and kiss. "Next door with the neighbor kids. They're eating over there, so I'm fixing dinner for just the two of us."

"Wow—that never happens. An adult dinner and conversation. I'm not sure what we do in this situation."

Gabriela poured them both a glass of wine. "How about we talk about your new job? Now that you've had a chance to meet these people, can you work with them?"

"I suppose. It's just like it was in Dallas. There are 25 people on the team, then there's this smaller group from the team that meets every month for dinner. They call it the Dinner Club. I suppose they're representative of the office. Some are motivated, and some are miserable."

"Anybody stand out?" Gabriela asked as she finished preparing dinner.

"The guy who asked me to join the group for dinner," Miles answered as he started setting the table. "His name is Sydney Wells. Great big guy with enough energy for three people. I like his enthusiasm."

"What about the others?"

"There's this one guy they call Mr. Doom-and-Gloom," Miles responded with a perplexed look on his face. "I have been around negative people before, but this guy is a master at finding the bad stuff and bringing it to the attention of anyone who will listen."

"He can't be *that* bad."

"Wait until you have the displeasure of meeting him before you draw that conclusion," Miles said as he shook his head.

After they bowed their heads and gave thanks for the meal, Gabriela and Miles continued their conversation about the new experience Miles was having. Then, hand in hand, they went next door to get the boys. Work was important to Miles, but nothing compared to his family.

ONE-ON-ONE

Miles found it hard to believe that January had come and gone. He figured he would see a little more of Seth than he had, but apparently getting settled into his new management job required some time out of the office.

Miles never really needed much from his managers. He was what the management gurus called "self-motivated." He never looked to a manager to provide the motivation to do something that should just be done. As he'd spent time getting to know some of the other people on his team over the past few weeks, he couldn't help but notice there were many people who seemed to be waiting for a little nudge to do their jobs. In fact, Miles was amazed at the number of people he met in his first month who seemed to show up to work, do the bare minimum needed to get by, collect a paycheck, and go home.

Miles realized Seth was back in the office after having been away for training as a new manager. Miles had just settled in at a computer station for the morning when a shift coordinator handed him a note asking him to go to Seth's office for a meeting.

"Good morning, Seth," Miles offered as he entered the small cubicle across from his computer station. "You asked to see me?"

Seth glanced up quickly as he shuffled through some papers on his desk. "Yeah, Miles. Come on in and take a seat."

After a minute or so, Seth turned around in his chair and began. "As I'm getting settled into my new job, I'm having one-on-ones with each member of my team, and you're one of the last ones I have to cover. I thought we could spend some time together this morning."

"Cool," Miles replied as he sat back in his chair.

Seth skimmed through what Miles assumed was his employee file. "I see you've been with Halifax for 20 years. It indicates here you were one of the best employees in the Dallas call center. Why would you want to make a change?"

Miles paused and shifted in his chair as he considered the best way to respond. Smiling, he said, "It's probably not the answer I should give my new boss, but I didn't like my boss."

"It must have been pretty bad to move across the state to get away from a bad boss. If you were one of the best, why didn't you just move to another team?"

"That was an option," Miles replied, "but I was just ready for a new start. My wife was ready for a change of scenery as well, and we thought this would be a nice place to move."

"It is a nice place to move. I've only been here a month now, but I could definitely get used to living here."

"So, how has your first month gone?" Miles inquired. "This is your first management job out of college, right?"

"Yes it is, and it hasn't been too bad. It's more work than I thought it would be, but I love it. It's taken most of the month to get settled into the job. Procedures to learn, reports to complete, meetings and training to attend, and amid all that, I have to find time to lead all of you. In time, I'll get it all figured out. I welcome the challenge."

"I've never been officially promoted to a management job during my career," Miles replied, "but I spent some time as an interim manager several years ago. If there is anything I can ever do to help, don't hesitate to let me know."

"I appreciate that. I just might take you up on your offer some day. Until then, I want to share with you an employee engagement initiative we're going through with Hannah."

"I heard something about that," Miles responded with a hint of curiosity and another shift in his chair. "What's it all about?"

"It's something Hannah has been sharing with the management team. Part of her mission in this office is to create a more engaged culture."

"I've only been here a month," Miles responded, "but I see a lot of disengagement."

"Apparently we're not different than most organizations. According to a study conducted by the Gallup Organization, three out of four employees are at some level of disengagement. The majority are just disengaged, but nearly 20 percent are *actively* disengaged."

Miles laughed out loud. "I've met a few of those people already. It's like they're constantly trying to get people to join their pity parties. I assume you've met Larry Marcus."

"I have. In fact, I've been saving Larry to the end. He will be my last one-on-one session later this morning."

Miles shook his head. "Good luck with that. I've had the chance to spend some time around him. He is perhaps the most negative person I've ever met. I'm sure that is feeding his disengagement."

"We're determined to overcome some of that. Hannah is introducing a model called *Engaged Leadership*. She hopes that if she can get the managers leading their teams with what we're learning, the employee engagement in this office will improve. And I'm hoping if I can get our team more engaged, then maybe we can get out of last place compared to the other three teams."

For the rest of their time together, Seth led a conversation that allowed Miles to share a little about his personal life. After a great conversation, Seth wrapped up the meeting and Miles stood to leave. As Miles got to the doorway, Seth said, "Oh, I almost forgot. We're doing an Employee Engagement Survey as part of this employee engagement initiative, so I need you to take some time to complete the survey. You'll be getting an e-mail with the link. We're trying to determine a benchmark for how the employees think we're doing as managers. I know you're new to the office, but provide whatever feedback you can on the survey."

With that, Miles headed back to his computer station. Along the way he thought about satisfaction surveys done in other offices over the course of his career. The employees were asked to take the time to complete the survey, and that was it. There was never any follow-up, and no one ever saw any changes. Miles hoped this time would be different.

MORE OF LARRY MARCUS

"Sucking up to the boss already," Larry quipped as Miles walked into the break room.

"Not at all. He called me in to have a one-on-one meeting. He's apparently doing them with everyone on our team, and you're coming up later this morning. Get ready, Mr. Doom-and-Gloom."

"Great. Now I have something to look forward to before lunch. So, how did it go?"

"Fine," Miles replied as he sat down at the table with Larry. "We spent some time getting to know each other, and then he explained some of the plans behind the employee engagement initiative."

"It's always tricky with a new boss," Larry replied peering over his glasses. "You have to figure them out. You know, figure out what you can get away with."

Miles stared at Larry for a moment before he responded. "You don't like to work, do you?"

"Of course not—who likes to work? That's why they call it *work*. Don't you remember learning early on that work was bad? Think about it. When you were a kid, it was all about fun until your parents came along and made you do home-*work*. When they weren't badgering you to do some work, they were complaining about their own jobs and how much they hated to work. So, no, Miles, I don't like to work."

"Sounds like you've put a lot of thought into it," Miles responded.

"Hey, man. It's just a job. They do what they can to get the most out of us, and we do what we can to avoid having to do it. Just show up and keep your eye on the prize—Friday."

Miles couldn't figure out if Larry didn't like work, or if he just didn't like management. Maybe it was something even bigger. Maybe he didn't like himself.

THE BEST AND THE BRIGHTEST

Miles had seen a lot of managers during his 20-year career at Halifax. Some were good, and some were really bad. Although he hadn't known Seth very long, Miles was impressed with this young man. There was something about him that just seemed to inspire people around him.

Sure, there were things he did that made a difference, like getting out of his office every morning and greeting employees at their computer stations. That was a nice touch. The fact he regularly informed employees of their performance throughout his first month and provided encouragement for them to do even better certainly didn't hurt. But perhaps the most significant aspect of Seth Owen was the indescribable charisma that just made people want to follow him wherever he was leading.

Miles was getting close to the end of his shift
when he got a note from a shift coordinator
instructing him to meet in the conference room
at 3:00 PM. Seth hadn't mentioned anything about
a team meeting during his one-on-one session, so
he didn't have a clue what the meeting was about.
When he walked in, he noticed he was one of six
members of his team. Sydney was there, along
with four other team members he recognized
from the introductions during the first team meeting in January.

"I've asked to meet with you because I need
your help," Seth started as he made eye contact
with each person in the room. "After meeting with
the entire team in the one-on-one meetings, I
consider you to be the best and brightest on
the team."

Miles had always been a top performer in any
office he'd worked, and he was glad Seth considered him one of the best. Then again, Miles had
seen the motivation level of most of the people
around him, so he knew the competition wasn't
that tough. He was certainly curious to see where
this meeting was going.

"Not only are you the top performers, but you
seem to be a group I can confide in. A change has
been made in the strategic plan of the organization, and I want to run it past you before I share
it with the entire team. The change affects how
we measure Representative Occupancy."

Miles had been in call centers for a long time,
so he knew that Representative Occupancy was

a term used to describe the amount of time a call center rep actually takes to handle customer calls, as opposed to nonproductive time like meetings.

Seth took some time to explain how a change in technology would result in a change in procedure. After he finished his explanation, he asked, "Can any of you think of a reason why this would not be good for the team?" Miles had some questions, as did some of his fellow team members. Seth did a great job answering their questions and settling their concerns. After he was finished, Seth asked, "Can I count on you for your support of the change?" Every head in the room nodded in support.

"Good. I anticipate we may have some on our team who won't agree with the change. I plan to meet with the entire team to share the changes later this month. Any help you can provide supporting the change will be greatly appreciated."

After the meeting, everyone went back to work. All except for Miles. His shift was over, and he headed home to his kids. Benjamin and Michael planned to participate in Little League Baseball later in the year, and Miles had promised to work with them long before the tryouts. On his drive home, he thought about those employees who would disagree with the changes. Regardless of how good the changes would be, Miles knew there would be some who would fight the change just for the sake of fighting change.

BRING ON THE COMPETITION

Miles was looking forward to the Dinner Club this month. Unlike for the January gathering, he was not going to be late this time. He arrived early, if for no other reason than that he refused to get stuck sitting next to Larry again. He felt certain his negativity could rub off on him like the flu, and he didn't want to be exposed to it again.

He thought he would be the first to arrive, but he was wrong. Larry and Deanna beat him to the table. When he thought about the actively disengaged employees Seth spoke about in his office earlier that week, Miles thought about Larry Marcus.

"Did you see the scoreboard they hung in the office?" Larry spouted with a frown as Miles approached the table. "They've listed all four teams, along with every area they measure. I hear they're going to update it every month to show which team is doing better in the office."

"Awesome," Miles said as he looked at the table to determine the best position to be in so he wouldn't get stuck talking with Larry all night. "A little competition should be good for us all."

"Uh, Miles, did you see where we fell in January?" Larry asked with a touch of sarcasm in his voice.

"I did not. I was off today."

"Well, we're in the same place we've always been," Larry responded. "Last place—in every aspect they measure."

"Who is 'they'? You keep saying 'they' did these things?"

"Management," Larry responded with an attitude.

"Sorry. I just thought we were all on the same team working toward the same goal. When you say the word 'they,' it just sounds like we're not a part of the same team."

"As far as I'm concerned, we're not," Larry growled.

Miles glanced over at Deanna, who simply looked perplexed by Larry's negativity. She just shrugged her shoulders. As Miles glanced back across the table at Larry, he recalled a quote he heard many years ago. "Never argue with an idiot. He'll just drag you down to his level, and then beat you with experience." Miles felt certain Larry had plenty of experience as an idiot, and decided there was no need to continue this conversation.

Just as he started to change the conversation to something a little less controversial, Sydney and Mattie walked through the door and headed to the table.

"Did you see the scoreboard?" Sydney asked as Miles sat down.

Here we go again, Miles thought to himself.

"No, I didn't," Miles responded. "Larry was just telling us all about it. Apparently 'they' are putting the heat on us by comparing the four teams in the office." Larry shot him a quick glare.

"That's not the board he's talking about," Mattie responded as she took off her coat and hung it on her chair. "You're talking about the 'Big Board.' Sydney's talking about the 'Little Board' Seth put up outside his office. It has all 25 of us on it, and it lists our personal performance in each category the office is tracking."

"Awesome," Miles responded as he looked across the table at Larry. "A little competition should be good for us all."

"Apparently we have some work to do," Sydney replied. "Our team is in last place in every category on the Big Board according to the January results."

"We all have some work to do if we're going to catch Aaron's team," Mattie responded. "As usual, they're in first place in every category again."

"We'll catch them," Miles responded, smiling at Mattie. "I welcome the competition."

"Enjoy yourselves," Larry said as he finished his margarita. "I'm out of here. Only two days until this rat has to get back in the rat race, so I'm going to go enjoy the weekend. I've got places to be."

He may have claimed he had some place to be, but Miles suspected he wanted to be anyplace but with people who thought a little competition was a good thing.

STEPPING UP

The office had been rather quiet for a few days. Seth had been away for some training. Upon his return, he called a meeting with the entire team. Miles suspected this would be the meeting to share the change to Representative Occupancy, and he was right. As he headed to the conference room, he felt somewhat special, because Seth had confided in him and a handful of fellow team members a few days earlier.

After everyone settled in, Seth began his explanation of the changes related to Representative Occupancy. As expected, a few people started to squirm in their chairs. Some people just can't stand change, Miles thought. After some discussion, two of his coworkers started to complain. After hearing their concerns, Miles took over.

"Before you go any further," Miles said. "I want to say I think this is a good change." He shared the reasoning for his opinion, and used his years of experience as credibility. When he was finished, a few of the others from the premeeting with Seth jumped in and added a few remarks. Before long, several of the normally quiet employees were agreeing with the change. The majority in agreement seemed to have silenced the naysayers. Miles didn't know whether that is what Seth had in mind when he solicited their support in advance of the meeting, but if he did, it had worked.

This was a good meeting for Miles. For the first time since his arrival at this new office, he was able to exhibit his influence in front of his team.

SPECIAL ASSIGNMENT

There were many things Miles liked about being able to have Gabriela stay home raising the boys. Perhaps one of his favorites was knowing she was able to prepare healthy meals for the family every day. As a boy, Miles could tell you the entire menu of the top three fast-food restaurants near his house without even looking at the menu. If it weren't for Gabriela, he could probably do the same at this point in his life.

On this particular day, Gabriela was volunteering at the church all day, and Miles offered to bring dinner home. He had been talking about how good the food was at La Cantina and had promised to take the family there for dinner. He decided to stop off and pick up dinner instead.

He walked in and ordered from the lady behind the counter. He was about to take a seat to wait for his order when he noticed Hannah and Seth at a corner table. About the same time, Seth noticed Miles, and he motioned for him to join them.

"Are you meeting anyone for dinner?" Seth asked as Miles approached the table.

"Not tonight. My wife has been busy all day, and I agreed to stop off and pick up dinner. I just put in my to-go order."

"Sit down and join us while you wait," Hannah said. "Your ears should have been burning. We were just talking about you."

"That can't be good," Miles laughed. "The two of you come to happy hour and talk about work?"

"We solve all the world's problems right here at this table," Seth responded.

"So, what were you talking about?" Miles asked.

"We're working on this employee engagement initiative, and we were discussing the employee's role in an engaged culture. We're wondering if anything we do as a management team can make much difference in a person's engagement level if they aren't happy in the personal aspects of their life—you know, like family, friends, health, money, all that."

Miles leaned back in his chair and responded, "That's a fair question."

"Of all the call center reps on my team, you seem to be one of the most engaged," Seth interjected. "Now, you're doing the same job as the other call center reps. Some of them are terribly disengaged, and yet you seem to enjoy your job. What makes you so engaged?"

Miles thought about the question for a moment. "Well, first of all, I can't fathom not making the best of the time I spend at work. I have to be there, so I'm going to choose to enjoy it."

"So, part of it is just how you choose to see work," Seth said, more as a statement than a question. "What about all the personal stuff in your life—that whole work/life balance thing? Do you have all that worked out?"

"I'm not sure I've ever gotten it all worked out," Miles laughed, "but at this point in my life, it's about as good as it's ever been. That hasn't always been the case though. Early in my career, I was just going through the motions at work. I thought it was just a job then. I attended one of those motivational seminars. There were several speakers, and one stuck out in my mind. I can't remember his name, but his message stuck with me."

"What was his message?" Hannah asked.

"The main point of his message was about the responsibility we have for our own satisfaction at work. I don't think it was the work/life balance thing, but it was about taking control of our own happiness. He talked about the different aspects of our life, and how addressing those areas could help make us happier at work."

"Did it work?" Seth asked.

"It did. I think there were four or five areas he talked about."

"Did the company send you to the seminar, or did you go on your own?" Seth asked.

"I went on my own. It was one of those full-day seminars with multiple speakers. I took the day off and stayed all day. They even had some special deal where you could sit in a special section up front and attend a private lunch with the speakers if you paid extra. I did it all. Classic overachiever, I guess."

"That brings us to what we were talking about before you got here," Hannah said. "We were discussing whether someone has to be self-motivated to achieve your level of engagement or whether it can be learned."

Miles thought about the comment for a moment before he responded. "I think it certainly helps if you're self-motivated, but I believe it can be taught. If someone's not aware of what they need to be working on in their life to be more satisfied, they can certainly learn from training."

"Halifax University offers a half-day seminar on life balance," Hannah responded. "We don't have it in our budget to send everyone to the training, but we could have the trainer come to the call center for two days and do a session for each of the groups."

"Makes sense," Miles replied. "I suppose it couldn't hurt."

"The problem is, we have no idea whether the session is any good or whether our employees would even respond to it," Seth replied. "I planned to attend to check it out, but I need to spend as much time as possible in the office with my team. Would you be willing to attend the session at Halifax University and let us know what you think?"

"I would be happy to do it," Miles responded, "but why not send another manager?"

Hannah was prepared for the question. "We want someone to look at this through the lens of the employee. We believe employees must contribute to the culture, and it's important that an employee believe this could make a difference."

"Fair enough. When would you want me to go?"

Hannah and Seth looked at each other and smiled. "That's the catch. They are offering a session this Thursday morning. You would have to fly up there tomorrow. You could be back home in your own bed Thursday night."

"Count me in," Miles replied with enthusiasm. "I'll work out the details with my wife and make arrangements to leave tomorrow. I'm bringing home dinner, so she should be in a good mood!"

PACK MY BAGS

Miles Freeman was the kind of person who seldom allowed his surroundings to get him down. Sure, he was human, but he knew his *reaction* to the events in his life had a much bigger impact than the actual events. Gabriela always expected Miles to come home in a good mood, but this evening he had even more energy than usual.

"Hey, Sweetie," Miles called out from the kitchen as he put the to-go bags from La Cantina on the counter. "Dinner is here."

The twins made it to the kitchen before Gabriela, and after a quick hello, they took what they dug from the bag and headed to the living room to eat their dinner.

"I guess we're not eating as a family tonight," Miles said to Gabriela as she walked over for her "welcome home" hug and kiss.

"Not tonight. The kids are working on a class project that's due tomorrow. We'll have dinner together tomorrow night."

"Actually, tomorrow night will not be good for me," Miles responded as he pulled the two remaining Styrofoam boxes from the bag. "I ran into Seth and Hannah at La Cantina, and they've asked me to help them with the employee engagement initiative."

"That's great. What have they asked you to do?"

"They want me to fly up to Halifax University tomorrow to attend a training session on life balance," Miles responded. "It would only be for a night."

"I'm not worried about that. The kids and I will be fine. I remember when you went to a seminar like that years ago. I wonder if it's still the same."

"That was 20 years ago. I'm sure it's changed."

"You're still wearing some of the same clothes from 20 years ago," Gabriela joked. "That hasn't changed."

"Hey, there's nothing wrong with my clothes. They may be 20 years old, but they're still in style. Some things never go out of style."

"The same may be true for lessons on life balance," Gabriela said. "You better get in there and get some of those old clothes packed."

BLACK TIE AFFAIR

Miles liked the early shift. Most of the people he enjoyed being around, primarily his friends from the Dinner Club, worked the earlier shifts. He enjoyed working with them, but he really enjoyed getting home early enough to spend time with the twins.

As was usually the case, Miles was working the early shift on this particular day the first week in March. It was the Monday after his return from Halifax University, and he was looking forward to sharing what he had learned with Seth and Hannah. He had just gotten into the call center and was getting settled into a computer station around 8:30 when he heard some of his coworkers laughing across the call center. As he turned to look in that direction, he saw Seth walking across the office wearing a tuxedo. With a white cloth draped over his arm and a silver tray full of dough-nuts, Seth was walking to the computer station of each of his employees, passing out doughnuts.

Most days were very quiet in the call center, so Seth's actions were creating quite a commotion, but everyone seemed to be enjoying it. Everyone but Carmen, who had emerged from her office with Hannah. As expected, an ear-to-ear grin could be seen on Hannah's face, but Carmen seemed rather miffed as she watched how the employees reacted to Seth. She stood behind Hannah with her arms crossed, making little effort to hide her lack of tolerance for what was happening.

Seth walked over to Miles and handed him a card. Miles had a customer on the line, but he looked down and read the card: "Enjoy your doughnut. This is my way of saying thanks for everything you do. You make me proud to be your leader!" Since Miles was on a call with a customer, he couldn't say any-thing to Seth. However, he nodded appreciation to Seth as he took a doughnut from the tray.

Deanna was sitting across from Miles that morning, and when he finished his call, he leaned forward and asked quietly, "What's this all about?"

"Take a look at the Big Board," she replied, nodding her head in the direction of the officewide scoreboard. "The February results were posted this morning. Our team moved into third place in attendance."

Miles had seen some managers go out of their way to show appreciation to their employees, but

nothing like what Seth had done with the doughnuts. In some ways it was just plain silly. But for a
team that had been starved for attention, Seth made
them feel special. Not only had he made his employees feel special, he had raised the bar for the other
managers in the office. This wasn't just a gimmick to
impress the boss. This was changing the culture,
and Miles could see it happening. So could one of
his fellow team members who sat across the call
center with a scowl on his face. It didn't matter what
happened to enhance employee engagement, Larry
Marcus was never going to accept the efforts Seth
was making to improve the team. Sad—truly sad.

ROOTING FOR MATTIE

"Smile," Miles said to Mattie as he walked into the
break room for lunch. "Why the sad face?"

Mattie looked up and smiled when she saw it
was Miles. "Hey, traveling man. Welcome back. I
don't have a sad face. I'm just a little preoccupied
right now."

"Something big happening today?" Miles asked
as he pulled up a chair and opened his lunch.

"I'm meeting with Seth at the start of my shift.
He wants to talk about my attendance issue."

"You picked a good day," Miles responded.
"You missed the celebration this morning. The
February results came out, and we moved from
last place to third. He ran around the office in a
tuxedo handing out doughnuts on a silver tray.
He's in a pretty good mood today."

"A tuxedo? I can't believe I missed that! He had better have saved me a doughnut. Anyway, I better get in there so I won't be late. Wish me luck."

"You'll do great," Miles responded. "I'm rooting for you. Sydney is rooting for you. You'll do fine. You haven't missed any time this month have you?"

"I haven't missed any time this year," Mattie replied proudly. "I went from having the worst attendance record of anyone on our team to perfect attendance in January and February."

"Then your conversation with Seth should go well. You contributed to our success in both January and February. Just remember, we're rooting you on."

THE DEVIL'S ADVOCATE

"I've only been around a few months," Deanna said as everyone arrived for Dinner Club, "but I've never seen a manager do something as crazy as walk around the office in a tuxedo handing out doughnuts."

"I can't believe I missed it," Sydney laughed. "I heard it was great. That's all anyone has talked about this week."

"I thought it was stupid," Larry replied as he peered at Deanna over his glasses. "It's an office. We're there to work. These shenanigans just create a distraction and hurt customer service."

"I thought it was great," Miles replied. "And Deanna, I've been around a *long* time, and I've never seen a manager do something as crazy as walk around the office in a tuxedo handing out doughnuts, either."

"I missed it, too," Mattie interjected. "But I did get my doughnut in a meeting with Seth later that day."

"That's right," Sydney said. "I forgot you were having your meeting with Seth this week. How did it go?"

"It went great. He thanked me for having a couple months of perfect attendance and offered to buy dinner for me and my husband if I go the next four months without an absence."

With his usual sour attitude, Larry had to provide his opinion, dripping with sarcasm. "Great, he's going to reward you for doing your job."

"I'll make it the next four months without an absence, but I'll do it because I want to, not because of the reward. Although I must admit, the reward is certainly nice."

As he scanned the menu, Miles commented, "By the way, Mattie and Deanna can't make it to Dinner Club next month on the first Friday of the month. Should we reschedule or just skip a month?"

"Let's just skip a month," Sydney answered. "April will be a busy month with Easter activities, so let's just wait until May to meet again."

Larry had been waiting to jump in. "I don't know why we keep coming here anyway. The service is lousy and the food is awful."

"Are you eating the same food we are?" Mattie asked. "This food is great, and if you didn't order a half dozen margaritas every time we come here, you wouldn't need a waiter every 10 minutes."

"This place is just terrible," Larry growled.

Miles had been holding back any comments related to Larry's constant negativity over the past several months, but he needed to confront him. "Larry, you seem to take pride in finding the negative aspect of everything. You don't like the service. You don't like the food. Every time we talk about the office you point out the negative aspect of whatever topic is in front of us. What's that about?"

"I'm a realist, Miles. Somebody around here has to look at the other side. I guess you can call me the devil's advocate."

"What makes you think the devil needs an advocate every time we get together?" Sydney asked.

"I just see all of you falling for this nonsense at the office, and I want you to see it for what it's worth."

"I see it as Seth trying to make things better for his employees," Miles responded. "The management team is committed to creating a culture of employee engagement, and you seem determined to knock it down every chance you get."

Larry had no reply. He just sipped his margarita and glared across the table at no one in particular.

Miles was on a roll. "In fact, have you ever considered that maybe you're hurting the culture around here with your negativity?"

"Don't try to pin this lousy culture on me."

"First of all, it's not a lousy culture for all of us. Second, I'm not trying to pin it all on you," Miles

responded. "I'm just trying to pin your own dissatisfaction on you."

Larry paused for a second before he began to
smile, an unfamiliar sight to anyone who knew
him. "Oh, that's right. You've been off to charm
school, haven't you? Been off listening to all that
motivational crud, sucking up to the boss. That's
where all this is coming from."

"Twenty years," Miles replied staring at Larry.
"Twenty years, and I've never met someone as
negative as you. My observation has nothing to
do with the training I attended. I just think we all
have a responsibility to contribute to the culture of
employee engagement, and it just seems that
maybe you're part of the problem."

When Larry got up from the table and walked
out of La Cantina without saying a word, Miles
wondered if Larry couldn't take the criticism, or if
he knew there might be a little truth to his observations. Miles figured there was a little of both.

WE HAVE SOME WORK TO DO

Miles didn't even know there was an auditorium in
the building. That morning Seth and Aaron held
a joint team meeting, and the auditorium was the
only meeting room in the building that could seat
50 people.

The purpose of the meeting was to share the
results from the Employee Engagement Survey
done the previous month. As it turned out, the
results weren't all that good. After reminding

everyone of the vision and mission statements of the office, Seth and Aaron took turns explaining the results of the survey. They explained that employees indicated they didn't know what was going on and that they didn't feel like they were being recognized. While most of the criticism was pointed at management, the results also showed that employees didn't feel others in the office were pulling their own weight.

"We have some work to do," Seth commented. "I suppose the managers could try to come up with ways to address the concerns in the survey, but we may miss the mark. We either know what needs to be done and we're not doing it, or we don't know what to do. Either way, we need to make some changes.

"Well said," Aaron offered. "With that in mind, we're putting together an Engagement Team to work on the areas of improvement. This feedback came from you, the call center reps, and the solutions should come from you as well. Anyone interested in working on this employee team to address the areas of concern from the survey should get in contact with me by Friday. I will be coordinating this group."

After the meeting, Miles headed to the call center for his shift. It was a slow afternoon, and the day seemed to drag on for many of the reps. Miles used the extra time to determine what he would present to Hannah and Seth. His shift was just about to end when a shift coordinator handed him a note. It read, "Looking forward to hearing about your training experience. At the start of your

shift tomorrow, meet me and Seth in the conference room.—H."

SHOWTIME

Miles was in the conference room long before
9:00 AM. He had put together his notes and was
preparing his remarks when Hannah and Seth
walked into the room.

Hannah didn't waste any time as she took a
seat. "Well, what did you think?"

"The training was good, but the travel wasn't so
great. Not sure why I got dressed before I went
to the airport since I had to get redressed after I
went through security."

"That travel thing isn't so glamorous, is it?"
Hannah smiled.

"Not at all, but it was worth it. The training
was great."

"Should we do it for the office?" Seth asked.

"I think we should, as long as we can get the
same trainer. There are two aspects to any training—
the message and the messenger. The message was
great, and so was the messenger. They may have
other great trainers, but this guy was really good."

"Give us an overview," Hannah directed. "Spare
us the details. I've been through these types of
seminars before. I just want to see the big picture."

"Sure. I've been through these types of seminars before as well, and quite frankly, it wasn't
much different from anything I've seen before. But
as with anything we ever learn, it isn't about

having the knowledge. When it comes to managing all the stuff in our lives, our success will not be determined by what we know. Our success will be determined by what we do."

"Fair enough," Hannah replied.

"In fact, as I sat through the program, I realized some things I don't do very well in my own life, and I think I do a pretty good job of finding balance. No matter where the call center reps are in their lives, they can learn something from this program. At the very least, they'll be reminded of some things they probably haven't done in a while."

"It was a half-day training, right?" Seth asked.

"Yes, and it was a good mix of lecture and exercise. In fact, most of the class was spent applying the concepts to our own lives. We had group discussions and personal application time. By the time we left, each person had completed a portion of a Personal Planning Sheet. We each were encouraged to take it home to finish."

"And you think it was good enough to bring the trainer here?" Hannah asked again.

"Absolutely. Again, even if they've heard it before, they'll be reminded of what they're not doing in their lives."

"Let's talk about you," Hannah responded. "You've said you think you do a pretty good job of maintaining balance in your life. Are there some things you'll do differently as a result of the training?"

"There are definitely some things I'll do differently. First of all, I'm going to stop trying to balance everything. I've been beating myself up trying to achieve this mythical balance, when what I should have been doing was finding a way to weave it all together. I plan to share what I learned with my wife, and I'm certain it will have an impact on her life as well."

"Good," Hannah replied, "then sending you to the training was money well spent. I appreciate you taking the time to go up to Halifax University to check out the program. The management team will discuss it, and you'll know soon enough whether we'll be doing it for everyone in the office."

A SAD LITTLE LIFE

Miles had just enjoyed an exceptional weekend. Gabriela had been feeling a little homesick, so they invited their best friends from Dallas to visit. Miles had taken the previous Friday off from work, so they were able to enjoy a nice three-day weekend with their friends. As was usually the case, Miles was looking forward to getting back to work on Monday.

As he walked into the break room, Miles saw his least favorite person sitting at a table reading the newspaper. Larry was the only person in the break room, so sitting at another table didn't seem like an option.

"Anything good in the paper today?" Miles asked as he poured his morning cup of coffee.

Miles didn't expect him to put the newspaper down, so he wasn't surprised when he didn't. "Never is."

"Then why bother reading it?"

"I like to know what's going on in the world, Miles," Larry responded as he folded the paper down and peered over his glasses. "Don't you read the newspaper?"

"Comics," Miles replied as he sat down. "I prefer to find something worth laughing about, particularly if I'm reading the newspaper first thing in the morning. Besides, I figure somebody like you will tell me if there's anything important I need to know."

"Have you bothered to look at our March results posted on the board?"

"I didn't know they were posted yet," Miles responded as he sat back in his chair. "Anything exciting?"

"Well, we're still in third place in attendance. We moved from fourth to third in a key quality measurement. No sign of any doughnuts or tuxedos, but I'm sure there will be some shenanigans to celebrate. I still don't know why they have to post that stuff for all the world to see."

"Maybe some people get inspired to see we're making progress," Miles responded.

"If they get inspired by that, then they're living a sad little life."

Miles spent a moment figuring out how to respond to Larry. "Did you do anything fun this weekend?"

"No," Larry responded with his trademark glare-over-the-glasses look. "Knocked around the house on Saturday, watched some television on

Sunday, and then started thinking about having to come back here today and be around all these people. Does my social life interest you, Miles?"

"No, I just assumed you always have big plans on the weekend. Every week you start your five-day countdown to the weekend like you've got something fantastic planned, but I never hear of anything fun you've done on a weekend."

"Doesn't have to be fun," Larry responded as he got up from the chair to head back to work. "Just has to be somewhere other than work. And speaking of that, my shift is about to start. Another long week of being around these sad little people living sad little lives—all in search of a little recognition."

Miles figured there was no way Larry could ever be happy at work when he wasn't even happy in his own life. He also couldn't help but think of the irony that the one person he saw living a sad little life would have the nerve to think others were living sad little lives.

A PRODUCTIVE MONTH

April was an especially productive month for the office. Miles knew the managers had another one of their quarterly meetings where Hannah shared the *Engaged Leadership* program, but he didn't have any idea what she was sharing. Regardless, Miles figured something must be working, because there was a lot of positive energy coming from the management team. Between what Hannah was sharing and the recommendations from the Engagement Team, there seemed to be a new energy level in the office.

Miles had just settled into a computer station when a shift coordinator handed him a note asking him to see Seth before he logged in for his shift.

"You wanted to see me, boss?" Miles said as he walked into Seth's office.

"Yeah, grab a seat. Two things. One, we're bringing the life balance trainer to our office. We're going to schedule the training for next month."

Miles took a seat across from Seth's desk. "Awesome. Are they sending the same trainer that I saw at Halifax University?"

"Yep. In fact, that's why we had to wait until May. He's apparently in demand. The other thing I wanted to talk to you about is our April results. I am going to be out of the office when the report is due at the end of the month, and I need you to check our team's results for accuracy and then turn in the report."

"Isn't all that stuff automated?" Miles asked.

"It is, but I like to review everything before it's submitted. The reports are easy to produce. In fact, it will only take a few minutes for me to show you how to log in and check them for me while I'm gone."

"I'm happy to do it," Miles responded. "With all the good energy I'm feeling this month, maybe this will be a great month for the team."

The truth would be in the numbers.

MIXED EMOTIONS

Miles had grown accustomed to getting text messages from Sydney, but he wasn't sure he had ever gotten one from Mattie. He had just pulled into the driveway after work when he felt his phone vibrate in his pocket. He stared at the phone for a moment before he realized it was Mattie's number, then read the simple message: CALL ME!!!!!!

Miles was brought up short by the capital letters and the multiple exclamation points. It was either really good news or really bad news, and Miles needed to know right away. He turned off the car and called Mattie immediately.

"You're not going to believe this," Mattie answered the phone with more enthusiasm than Miles had ever heard from her. "Aaron just called to tell me our team took over the number one spot in attendance in April."

Miles was just about to react when he realized his mistake. Seth had asked him to turn in the team's results while he was off at training, and he had completely forgotten to do it. He struggled trying to remember what happened, and he realized that nothing in particular had caused him to forget. He simply forgot to do it, and he knew he had let Seth down.

"Are you there, Miles?" Mattie asked.

"Yeah, yeah—I'm here. I was just a little preoccupied. Who did you say called you to give you the news?"

"Aaron," Mattie replied.

"Why would Aaron call you with the news?" Miles asked as he got out of the car to head inside.

"Because Seth is out of town. He has been at Halifax University, and he's flying back tonight. Aaron and Hannah are meeting him to share the good news."

"No, I mean *why* would he call you with the news?" Miles asked again. "Won't Seth just post the results on the Big Board tomorrow?"

"He called me because he thought we might want to do something to surprise Seth tomorrow when he comes to work. I was thinking we could do a banner or something to put in his office, but I don't want to do it by myself. Come help me put it together."

"Sure," Miles answered as he stared at his watch for a moment. "As soon as I get done with dinner, I'll text you to let you know I'm on my way."

Miles had always prided himself on being the responsible one. Other people drop the ball. Other people don't follow through on their responsibilities. Other people forget things. Miles Freeman was not one of these people, and for the rest of the evening he kicked himself for forgetting to turn in the team's results. At some point he'd have to face Seth to explain himself, and Miles was not looking forward to that conversation.

CONGRATULATIONS!

Mattie had sent a text message to everyone on the team inviting them to help with the banner, and at the least, to stop by and sign it. Although it may have been the team's results that made the difference, they knew it was Seth's leadership that really made the difference. A team doesn't go from last place to first place in a few months without influence from the leader, Miles thought to himself.

Although Miles had helped with the banner the night before and had already signed it, he showed up a little earlier than normal to help hang it in Seth's office. Once it was up and he had enjoyed his morning ritual of coffee in the break room, Miles settled into a computer station.

Not long after he started his shift, he looked up and saw Seth walk through the door. He saw the smile on Seth's face as he read the handmade banner hanging in his office: "Congratulations!"

Mattie and Deanna sat at computer stations close to Seth's office so they could see his expression when he came in, and they gave him the thumbs-up sign as he walked through the office. It was obvious to Miles that Mattie and Deanna were clearly happier in this engaged culture than they had been in the one before Seth arrived.

While Miles enjoyed the engaged culture as much as Mattie and Deanna, he did not enjoy the thought of having to face Seth with his explanation for dropping the ball.

FACING THE MUSIC

"I have some apologizing to do," Miles said to Seth as he walked into his cubicle.

Seth looked up, and when he noticed it was Miles, motioned for him to sit down without saying a word.

"You asked me to turn in the team's results while you were off at training, and I dropped the ball. I wish I had some grand excuse, but the truth is I simply forgot. I'm sorry for that."

Seth leaned back in his chair and said, "I appreciate you coming to apologize, and the apology is accepted. Jill called me and told me she hadn't received our results, and I assumed the office results would be delayed. Aaron took care of it for us, so everything was turned in on time."

"I'm glad Aaron helped you out, which seems rather ironic since our team just knocked his out of first place. But I still feel bad about letting you down."

Seth leaned forward in his chair. "Miles, you are one of the best reps in this call center, and there is no way I would let a simple mistake let me down. I'll admit I was a little let down at first because I thought perhaps there was some other reason you didn't get it done. But if it was a simple oversight, I'm okay with that. We all make mistakes, and as long as we're working every day to get better, don't worry about it this time."

"I appreciate your understanding. And by the way, congratulations on getting the team to first place in attendance."

"Wasn't me," Seth responded. "It took the 25 members of this team to come to work to improve our ranking in the office."

"True, but you created a culture where we wanted to be better, and that makes a big difference. I've worked with a lot of managers over the years, and at the risk of seeming like a brown-noser, I think you're doing a lot better after a few months than any I've ever met."

Miles knew it was weird to be praising his boss. The average employee usually doesn't do that, but Miles wasn't the average employee.

FINALLY FRIDAY

"I didn't think Friday would ever get here," Deanna said as she flopped down in her chair at La Cantina. "I am exhausted."

"You sit in a climate-controlled building all day handling calls in a call center, Deanna," Larry said as he glared over his glasses. "You get exhausted from *that*?"

Deanna would be the last person in this group to say anything bad to her friends—or anyone for that matter—but a part of her hoped Larry would not come back after he had stormed out of the last Dinner Club. "It's not just the work, Larry. I've got a life outside of Halifax."

"I've noticed you haven't been yourself lately," Mattie responded. "What's up with you?"

"Just some family stuff."

"What kind of family stuff?" Mattie asked.

"My grandmother is having hip surgery in a few weeks, and I'm just nervous for her."

"How long will she be in the hospital?" Sydney asked.

"Just for the day. She thought she would be in for three or four days, but she found a doctor who can do it in a day. Pretty amazing. She's trying to be tough, but I can tell she's scared."

"Are you going to go with her to hold her hand through it all?" Sydney asked.

"I can't."

"Why not?" Miles asked.

"I just started working at Halifax this past November. I can't take any time off until I've completed six months. The surgery is next month, but it is three days before my six-month anniversary with Halifax."

"You just need to talk to Seth," Miles responded. "Turn in a vacation request and explain the situation. I bet he'll make an exception."

"I just don't want to get in trouble during this probationary period."

"You won't get in trouble for asking," Mattie responded, "and it's not like you work for Carmen. She'd run you out of her office for even thinking about it. Just talk to Seth and see what he has to say."

Deanna thought back to the manager she had when she started in November, and knew she wouldn't have considered asking her for the favor. She knew Seth was different, and she hoped her friends were right.

TRAINING DAY

Halifax had invested a lot of money in its corporate training facility, known as Halifax University. Miles always appreciated the opportunity to attend training, but he really enjoyed being able to get away to Halifax University. The state-of-the-art training facility was nice, with no expense spared for technology. Since the company was bringing the life balance training to the office, Miles wondered how the local accommodations would compare.

It turned out there was no comparison. The company had leased the building for this relatively new call center, and the training room was simply a large space that had been reserved for future expansion of the call center. It was okay, but nothing compared to Halifax University.

Miles assumed he would not be included in the training since he had already gone through the program at Halifax University, so he was surprised when Seth asked him to join his team for the training. Seth had explained he wanted him to go through the training because he thought Miles might get something different from the training this time since he wasn't there to critique the class.

Carmen's team had gone through the training that morning, and Seth's team was scheduled for the afternoon. When Miles arrived in the training room after lunch, he noticed there were five tables— each with five chairs. The first thing he did was look for name tags. None. Whew! Although he knew assigned seating at training was probably better since it forced everyone to get to know other people—and it cut down significantly on low-level chatter—Miles always preferred to sit where he wanted.

He saw Sydney and Deanna sitting at one of the tables in the front, and he walked over to put down his notebook at their table to save his spot. He recognized the trainer, Dennis Riley, and went up to say hello. When he got back to the table, Mattie had arrived.

"You better find a fifth person to join us at our table, or Mr. Doom-and-Gloom will be wandering over here," Mattie laughed as she looked up at Miles and handed him a tent card with his name already written on it.

"I'm not too worried about that," Miles responded as he placed the tent card in front of his notebook. "I haven't gotten the impression lately he wants to spend much time with us."

Miles really wasn't worried about Larry joining the table, but the thought of spending the afternoon with him—in a life balance training of all places—was more than Miles wanted to consider. He waved over another team member and asked him to join the table, just to be safe.

LET THE LEARNING BEGIN

Miles remembered many things about the training session—and in particular the trainer—at Halifax University. One of the most significant was that Dennis started on time. There were still people in the hallway when 1:30 finally arrived, but he started on time.

"The story is old, and some of you may have heard it before. However, it's so appropriate today I'd like to start by sharing it. It's the story of an old dog lying on a front porch. A neighbor approached the porch and could hear the dog softly moaning. He asked his friend why the dog was whimpering. The owner said, 'He's lying on a nail.' Predictably, the man asked, 'Well, why doesn't he move?' To which the owner replied, 'I guess it doesn't hurt that much yet.'"

Miles had heard that tired old story years ago, but like most of the people in the room, he chuckled just like he did every time he heard it. A part of him wondered if he laughed because it was humorous or because he sometimes saw himself as the old dog.

"By a show of hands, how many of you know people like that old dog?" Dennis asked as he looked around the room and counted about half the participants. "These people complain about whatever situation they're in at the moment, but they don't do anything about it. You don't need to raise your hand for this next question, but how many of you have been that old dog at some point in your life? And if you are honest enough to admit to yourself that you've been that old dog, just how bad does the pain have to get before you get up and move?"

The last of the stragglers had slipped quietly from the hallway and into their chairs. "You see, a lot has been said about life balance, but apparently not much has been done, because most people will tell you they don't have much balance in their life. Sadly, many aren't willing to do anything about it. My hope is that we can change that for some of you this afternoon."

Miles waited a moment for Mr. Doom-and-Gloom to make a comment during the pause, and he thought Larry just might surprise him. No luck. Miles just hadn't waited long enough.

"Why don't you change it for all of us this afternoon?"

Dennis scanned the room to identify the person who asked the question. "Because some of you won't buy into what I have to say. I know this is a mandatory training session, and some of you in this room don't want to be here. Sadly, some of you entered the doors to this room assuming this would be a waste of time, and as a result, you won't buy in. I don't know who you are, but I know some of you won't agree with the importance of contributing to a culture of employee engagement."

Larry managed to find a new friend to wallow around in his misery during the training. He was sitting next to him, and Miles recognized him as one of his fellow team members who worked the night shift. He thought his name was Roger, but he wasn't sure. Like Larry, he hadn't put his name on his tent card. Miles figured this was their way of rebelling for having to attend the training.

"What do you mean by 'contributing to a culture of employee engagement'?" Larry's new friend asked with a frown. "I thought this class was about life balance."

"What is your name?" Dennis asked. "You didn't put your name on your tent card. Do you need a marker?"

Miles could see the marker on the table, and he figured Dennis could see it as well. Miles assumed this was the trainer's way of letting them know he recognized the game that was being played by the ones who didn't want to be in the room.

"My name is Roger," he answered, "and no, I don't need a marker. I have one right here."

"Well Roger, this class *is* about managing the aspects of your life. However, if you can increase your own life satisfaction by balancing your life, you'll be contributing to a culture of employee engagement. Consider it a nice by-product of figuring out how to bring more satisfaction to your life."

"My job is to do my job," Larry remarked. "It is management's job to get me excited about working here. If they want some 'engaged' culture, maybe you should be teaching them something today."

"Larry, employee engagement is a two-way road. Yes, great leaders recognize the need to build a culture of engagement by creating an environment where people want to come to work. But at the same time, employees must do some things to bring their own engagement to the table. Without both sides doing their part, employee engagement doesn't have a chance to work. So, our focus today will be on how we increase life satisfaction by addressing the multiple aspects of our lives, which in turn contributes to employee engagement."

Miles could tell Dennis was enjoying the challenges being thrown out by Larry and Roger, but he also knew it was cutting into the training program Dennis had planned. Miles had his weaknesses, but a lack of directness was not one of them. Looking over his shoulder toward their table behind him, he said, "Do you think you guys can hold your questions until later so we can get on with the training?"

Predictably, Larry glared over the rim of his glasses to show his disapproval.

IT'S NOT ABOUT BALANCE

Dennis nodded in Miles's direction as if to thank him for moving things along. "There are three things I want you to know before we get going this afternoon. First, I plan to ask a lot of questions to get you thinking. And I plan to put you to work, so I need you to participate. If you thought this afternoon's training session would be an opportunity to nap, I'm afraid you were wrong."

Dennis looked around the room to see whether he had gotten anyone's attention. "Second, I plan to share information you should already know. My experience has shown me that just because you know it does not mean you're doing it. And third, although you're in a life balance class, I'm going to encourage you not to balance your life."

"That's brilliant," came the sarcastic comment from Roger.

Dennis must have grown accustomed to that response to his comment because he didn't acknowledge Roger's remark or even look in his direction. "You see, balance is—by definition— an equality of distribution. When you consider the aspects of life, we will never have an equal distribution, and to pursue this mythical idea of balance simply brings frustration."

Looking around the room, Dennis paused for a moment to let the idea sink in. He walked over to a flip chart and turned back a few pages to reveal the model.

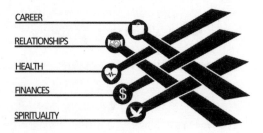

"Rather than thinking about life satisfaction coming from your ability to balance the many aspects of your life, I want you to consider that life satisfaction is more about weaving the most important things in your life together. It's represented by this woven fabric. You'll never have perfect balance between the five aspects of your life represented in this model because you have different priorities at different points in your life, so let's do ourselves a favor and not even pursue that myth."

"So, everything we've ever been told about trying to balance our lives is wrong?" Larry questioned cynically, continuing his challenge.

"I suppose to a certain degree it's more about semantics than anything else. I'm not trying to start a movement against life balance. I'm just trying to get you to think about life satisfaction as being more than just balance. You see, the more these five elements are woven and stitched together, the stronger the cloth—and our lives. Likewise, if one of the strands becomes loose, such as ignoring or pushing aside something in your life, it affects the whole piece. And if one of the strands is too tight, such as focusing on one aspect of your life too much, it affects the whole piece as well."

"Okay, I buy the idea of weaving the different aspects together instead of balancing them all," Sydney responded. "In fact, I think it makes more sense than balance. Balance sounds good, but I'm not sure any of us ever get there. You keep mentioning five aspects. What are they?"

CAREER

"I'm glad you asked," Dennis smiled as he looked at the projector screen. He clicked the forward button on his laptop remote control, and the woven image appeared on the screen with the word *Career*.

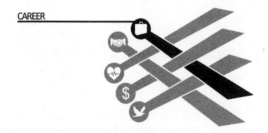

He turned back to face the group. "The first of the five aspects is *Career*, the reason you're all here at

Halifax. Then again, maybe some of you aren't here for a career. Maybe some of you are just here for a job. Can anyone tell me the difference between the two?"

No one volunteered to give a response. Miles had been through the course and knew the answer, so he decided to offer a response to get things going. "A career is a long-term commitment, something you've chosen to pursue because of a passion or particular interest. A job has a short-term horizon, something you do to earn an income to pay the bills."

"Well said," Dennis responded with a nod. "When I think of a job, I think of a discrete period of employment. There isn't much of a long-term attachment, because it's just something you have to do to get by—similar to several jobs I had in college to help me pay my bills. I did what I needed to do to get paid, and I couldn't wait for my shifts to end."

"I feel your pain," Larry remarked as he looked over at Roger and laughed.

"A career, on the other hand, should be something planned out and based on your interests. It's built throughout your lifetime, and should use your talents."

"I'm pretty sure we're all here because we have to work," Roger offered as he looked around the room to rally support. "We just have to live with it. They're all just jobs."

"Some people believe that," Dennis responded, "and it's unfortunate. You see, most people don't have the opportunity *not* to work. Jobs are often uninspiring and mundane, and careers can be exciting and challenging. Given the choice, I think most people would prefer a career. Your view of work and its connection to life will determine whether you see your work as a job or a career. And ultimately, that will determine your level of satisfaction with work."

"I'm telling you," Roger offered again, "they're all just jobs."

Deanna had been thinking a lot about this issue before it was ever brought up as part of the training. She hadn't known what she wanted to do for a living when she'd gone off to college and hoped she'd figure it out while she was there. After two years, she still hadn't figured it out, so she'd left college and decided to start working.

"I guess it all depends on how you view work for yourself," Deanna offered. "I've been at Halifax for just six months, and I'm trying to figure out what my career will be. Right now, this is a job for me because I'm in search of a career. But I've been talking to some of my friends and watching the people I work with around here at the company, and it seems there are two different types of people. Some see their jobs as a means to fulfill their financial needs, and they separate work from their personal life, and others see their jobs as a series of career moves that lead them to do something they like and that fits into their life—instead of being separate."

"I'm not sure many people ever find a career where they get to blend it all together into one happy life," Sydney replied.

"That may be true," Deanna responded as she turned toward Sydney at the table, "but the thought of dragging through—day after day—without some sense of real enthusiasm for my work seems unbearable. And quite frankly, I see some people in our office who live that way. What makes it even worse, some of these people have been here 25 years."

"Thank you for sharing your thoughts," Dennis responded. "It makes sense that people drag themselves to jobs when they see it as a way to pay the bills, much like I did in college. Unfortunately, there are many people who drag themselves through an entire career, when they have the power to control their own job satisfaction. So, whether you see your work as a job or a career, there are things you can do to take control of your own satisfaction as it relates to work. Although there are many, I'm going to share with you the two lessons in this program related to *Career*."

Dennis turned toward the screen and clicked the forward button on his remote.

Challenge One
Address the
hard questions
about your
career.

He turned back to the class and said, "Each of you will determine whether the work you do in your lifetime is a series of disconnected jobs required to pay the bills or a strategy required to do something you love to do. However, to get to the point where work actually contributes to your overall happiness, you need to ask some hard questions related to your career."

"Like whether or not we're happy in our career?" Mattie asked.

Dennis turned toward Mattie and replied, "That's certainly part of it. There are other legitimate questions to ask. In fact, the question I want to give you is this: Are you giving it your all? It may seem like a simple question, and most people would immediately answer yes. But if they stopped long enough to seriously answer the question, they may find they aren't really giving it their all."

"That's true," Mattie responded. "There were times when I worked for another manager in the office—who will remain nameless—and I would claim to be doing my best, but deep down I knew I wasn't really giving it my all. I mean, I don't think the team's performance would have been hurt much if I wasn't there. In fact, at some points it probably would have gotten better. That's not easy to admit, but it's the truth."

Miles pushed the process along. "Okay, we have a specific example for this one as we ask and answer the hard questions about our career. You mentioned there are *two* lessons related to *Career*. What's the second?"

Dennis turned toward the screen and clicked the forward button on his remote.

Challenge Two
Focus on your own personal growth.

He turned back to the group and said, "You are very fortunate to work for a company dedicated to employee development. Not all companies offer the level of training provided by Halifax. But I'm curious—if you didn't work for a company that offered training opportunities, would you seek out your own training?"

"Why would we?" Larry asked. "It's the company's job to train us if they want us to improve. If they aren't willing to pay for the training, I'm not going to use my own money to do something the company isn't willing to do."

"So you wouldn't invest in yourself if the training would help you in ways that might benefit you beyond your current job?" Deanna asked. "I mean, I want to figure out the right career path for me to take, and if Halifax isn't offering a class for that, I'd be willing to go find something to help me with that."

"Each of us in this room has a responsibility to focus on our own personal growth," Dennis responded. "There are many ways to do that, but one specific piece of advice I want to provide is this: Pursue training offered by your company. I know this may seem obvious, but you are wasting opportunities if training is offered—like this course—and you aren't taking advantage of it. In fact, no manager should ever have to make this type of training mandatory. Focus on your personal growth by pursuing the multitude of training opportunities offered by the company."

Dennis looked down at his watch and said, "Let's move on to the second aspect."

RELATIONSHIPS

Dennis turned to the projector screen and clicked the forward button on his remote control, and the woven image returned to the screen, this time with the word *Relationships*.

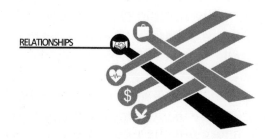

"The second aspect is *Relationships*, and this one is big," Dennis continued. "As humans, we crave good relationships. So it's ironic that we do so little to enhance the relationships with the people in our lives. It's as though we always expect someone else to do something to improve our relationships."

"Are you talking about relationships at home or work?" Miles asked.

"I'm talking about relationships in general," Dennis replied. "We'll talk specifically about work relationships in a moment, but right now I'm talking about relationships in general. Keep in mind the relationships in our personal lives often need more work than the ones in our professional lives."

"Why do you think relationships are such a struggle?" Deanna asked.

"That's a great question," Dennis replied. "I think we're so consumed with living our frantic lives that we just don't take the time to work on relationships. I also think that relationships change over time, and both parties in a relationship don't necessarily change at the same rate. But I'm absolutely certain that by improving our existing relationships or adding new relationships, we can experience a dramatic improvement in life satisfaction."

"Sometimes we have to eliminate unhealthy relationships to have the most impact," Mattie responded.

"Very true," Dennis replied. "As with the *Career* aspect, there are many things that can be done to improve in this area. However, I'm going to share with you the two lessons in this program related to *Relationships*."

All eyes turned to the screen as Dennis brought up the next slide.

"Who in this room would agree that we become like the people we're around?" Dennis asked as he looked around the room. Nearly every hand was in the air.

"Good. Then, with that in mind, how many people do you think consider that little fact when they determine who they hang around with? If we become like the people we're around, then we need to do an honest assessment of the people in our lives. Who are they? Are they adding to our lives or taking away? Do they lift us up or hold us down? Is their desire to achieve great things rubbing off on us, or are we wallowing around in a pool of mediocrity with them? And, whatever the answers to these questions may be, are you okay with the answers?"

There was an awkward silence in the room for a moment before Sydney made his comment: "I can think of some people—both at home and at work—who are not adding anything to my life. Are you saying I need to abandon everyone who doesn't add something to my life?"

"I'm not saying that at all," Dennis replied. "There are three things I hope you get from this discussion. One, you need to do an honest assessment of the people around you to determine whether any of them may be the reason you don't have the level of life satisfaction you want. Two, you need to determine what adjustments need to be made in order to spend more time around the people who will build you up. And three, you need to determine what you can do to help those who aren't adding anything to your life. Maybe they're in your life for you to help lift them up. So, no, I'm not saying you need to abandon everyone who doesn't add something to your life."

"That should bring you a little relief, Larry," Miles joked as he turned around to look directly at his table. "You must have thought you wouldn't have any friends left in this group."

As usual, any quick wit from Larry was substituted with a glare over his glasses.

"There are many actions you can take related to surrounding yourself with the right people, and the one specific action I want to share is this: Analyze your crew. People will come and go in your life, and you'll add new friends along the way. But one of the first things you should do is look at the people you're around today and see if you have people who support you."

Sydney pushed the process along this time. "Okay, so we surround ourselves with the right people, and we start by analyzing our crew. What's the next lesson related to *Relationships*?"

Dennis turned toward the screen and clicked the forward button on his remote.

Challenge Four
Enhance work
relationships.

"Let's talk about the relationships you have with each other here at the office," Dennis started as he put down his remote. "Your relationships here can have a huge impact on how much you enjoy where you work."

"I have plenty of friends," Larry remarked, "and I don't need to make more friends at work. In fact, I intentionally don't make friends at work so that

I can just go in and get my job done. The quicker I can get it done, the sooner I can get off work and go home to my real friends."

"That explains a lot," Miles chuckled as he looked around the table at his friends from the Dinner Club.

"Plenty of people would agree with your position, Larry," Dennis replied, "particularly if they see their work as a job and not a career. However, some of the happiest people I know are those who have established strong relationships with people at work."

"I'll stick with the ones in my personal life," Larry mumbled stubbornly.

Dennis clarified his point. "Keep in mind that enhancing the relationships you have at work is about more than just picking friends. It also includes how you act as an employee. With that in mind, I would like to offer the following specific action: Do what you say you're going to do. For many people, work relationships are more about being dependable than about friendliness. So, if you want to enhance work relationships, become known as a dependable person by doing what you say you're going to do."

Dennis looked at the clock on the wall and said, "Okay, we've gone through two of the aspects. Let's take a 15-minute break, and then we'll get started with the third aspect."

HEALTH

As he promised, Dennis was ready to start at the conclusion of the 15-minute break. Miles looked

up at the screen and noticed the third aspect was
already displayed: *Health.*

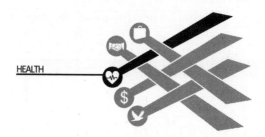

"The third aspect is *Health.* This is perhaps
the most overlooked aspect of our lives. The
importance of good health is widely known, and
I doubt anyone would try to minimize its
importance."

"Shouldn't it just get lumped in with the 'life'
portion of work/life balance?" Mattie asked.

"That's part of the problem," Dennis replied.
"Many people try to just lump it into the bigger
picture, but it requires our undivided attention.
Much of the dissatisfaction people feel in their
lives comes from living an unhealthy lifestyle."

"It's hard to give the appropriate time to focusing on health issues," Mattie said. "We live in a
quick-and-easy world. When you have two parents
working jobs, there isn't much time to prepare
nutritious meals. It's easier to just grab something
quick to eat."

"That's a valid point," Dennis replied, "but
keep in mind that health is more than just physical. Emotional health is important as well. Having
said that, there are two things you can do to take

control of your own satisfaction as it relates to health. I'm going to share with you the two lessons related to *Health.*"

Dennis clicked the forward button on his remote.

Challenge Five
Focus on your physical health.

"Let's continue with the discussion of physical health," Dennis started. "Consider this fact— two-thirds of Americans are overweight. Half of those are obese. It should come as no surprise that poor physical health translates into poor work performance. If we don't eat right and focus on our health, then chances are high we don't feel good at work. If we don't feel good, we aren't producing. When we aren't producing, we become disengaged from our work."

"I'll be the first to admit it," Sydney said. "I'm part of that obese statistic. I'm a pretty good employee, and my results show it, but I sometimes wonder how good I could be if I weren't tired all the time."

"Like all the other challenges, there are many ways to tackle this one, and many of them are obvious. We have all heard the advice a million times: Eat less, exercise more. Some people have medical reasons for their weight challenges, but the average person simply doesn't do the basics. For this one, the specific action I will give you is this simple: Learn about nutrition, and practice it."

Miles pushed the process along. "Okay, so we focus on our physical health, and we start by learning about nutrition and practicing it. What's the next lesson related to *Health*?"

Dennis advanced to the next slide.

Challenge Six
Focus on your
emotional
health.

"We've already discussed the importance of relationships, but I want to tie it to the focus on our emotional health. A key to enhancing our emotional health will be tied to the company of others. As social creatures, we have emotional needs for relationships. In order to feel and be the best we can, we must have positive connections to others."

"Sometimes I do best if I just deal with my issues alone," Deanna responded.

"You may feel that way at times," Dennis replied, "but we were not created to survive in isolation. We may have past experiences that have caused us not to trust people around us, and those experiences may even cause us to push others away. But we are wired to yearn for companionship, and it's a big part of our emotional health."

"That's true," Deanna responded, "but sometimes people just don't know how bad others have it in their lives."

"I can't argue with that," Dennis nodded. "In fact, it ties into the specific action I want to share: Keep it all in perspective. We all have challenges that affect our emotional health. We worry about things that have happened, and we worry about things that never will. But in the end, we should always know that somewhere in the world, someone is struggling with something even bigger. If you want to work on your emotional health, keep it all in perspective."

FINANCES

Dennis turned to the projector screen and brought the weave image back to the screen, this time with the word *Finances*.

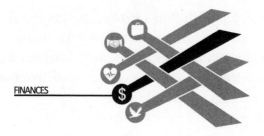

FINANCES

"The fourth aspect is *Finances*. This is one of the most taboo points to discuss. People will tell us if they don't like their jobs, and they'll wear us out complaining about their relationships. But, for whatever reason, finances are just not addressed in most circles."

"I agree with that comment," Sydney replied, "but why isn't this considered a part of career?"

"Several reasons. One, it's such a significant focus for a lot of people that it needs to be considered separately. Two, our finances are about much more than just the money we earn. The subject is also about how we *manage* the money we earn, and that shouldn't be confused with our career. And three, finances affect the other aspects of life balance. A struggle with finances almost always impacts a career. Some people will simply worry about their financial situation while on the job, and others will change jobs for more money—often without regard to life satisfaction. A struggle with finances almost always impacts relationships. Money has been the leading cause of divorce for many years. A struggle with finances can impact health. Some people stop eating and others lose sleep worrying about their situation. And a struggle with finances can impact spirituality. Some people start losing faith in anything—or anyone—other than themselves when they have financial problems."

Dennis reached over and picked up his remote. "So, let's take a look at the two things you can do to take control of your own satisfaction as it relates to *Finances*."

Challenge Seven
Tie financials to
your bigger
goals.

"People work for different reasons," Dennis remarked as he turned back to the audience. "Some work to earn an income, some work to keep themselves busy, and some work because they have a passion for the task. But the clear majority work to pay the bills. Would you agree?"

"Absolutely," Roger exclaimed. "I don't show up here every day for the pure joy of talking to these customers, and I sure don't show up here every day for the company of good friends."

"So, whether it's a job or a career for you, the money is your motivator," Dennis said more as a statement than a question.

"They're all just jobs," Roger repeated from earlier in the discussion.

Dennis was very good at stepping over the useless comments made in the training session and not allowing the naysayers to receive the attention they were hoping for. "Money is a motivator for most people. Regardless of your lifestyle, you have to pay the bills. But beyond the bills, all areas of your life have a tie to your money, so you must find a way to tie your financials to your bigger goals. The specific action I want to share with you today is this: Stop comparing yourself to those around you. When they try to keep up with someone else, too many people lose focus on using their financials to meet their bigger goals."

Mattie interrupted. "I agree. My husband and I do a pretty good job with our money, but you can't imagine how many things he buys because his buddies buy them. He's always trying to keep up with someone else, and quite often they make a lot more money than we do. If he would stop comparing himself to others and trying to keep up, we could focus our financials on our bigger goals."

"Well said," Dennis agreed. "Let's look at the next lesson related to *Finances*."

Challenge Eight
Add more value
to your
employer.

"How many of you would like a raise?" Dennis asked with a smile. Every hand was up in the air. Larry and Roger had both hands in the air.

"How many of you believe we are all here to add value to Halifax?" Dennis continued. He couldn't tell if every hand went up, but he knew most of the hands were in the air.

"I'm guessing the leadership of the company would hope we all believe we're here to add value to the company," Miles added.

"They would," Dennis replied. "Many employees will tell you they are underpaid. Like all of you, they want a raise. But not many employees stop to think about what is required for that to happen. You see, we each must be adding value."

"I just assume if I'm doing my job I'm adding value," Mattie said. "So, how does the company determine when we get a raise?"

"These types of decisions are made based on the financial performance of the company," Dennis replied. "Many factors are included in the financial statements, but in a nutshell, it's pretty simple. The company offers a product or service to sell. The company brings in income from the sale of the product or service; it pays the bills of the company; and, ultimately, it seeks to make a profit."

"So, if Halifax is profitable then we should get a raise, right?" Roger asked.

"Not necessarily," Dennis replied. "The company is seeking a profit for the investors of the company. It will not just give the profit to the employees, who are paid to do their job."

"Then how do we ever get a raise?" Larry interjected.

"By adding value to the company," Miles answered as everyone turned to look at him. "It goes back to the question Dennis asked about adding value to the company."

"So, how do we add value to the company?" Sydney asked.

"There are several ways you can do it, but the one I want to share is this: Find ways to make or save money for the company. It's all about revenue and expense. Find ways to add more revenue or reduce expense, and you've added value to the company."

SPIRITUALITY

Dennis clicked the forward button on his remote control to reveal the woven image and the final aspect, *Spirituality*.

SPIRITUALITY

"The fifth and final aspect is *Spirituality*."

"Here we go," Larry countered as he threw his hands in the air. "We're going to start talking about religion. I knew it was coming."

Dennis looked around the room to see what other reactions might be coming from the group before he responded. "*Spirituality* is a word with many meanings. Depending on how you were raised or where you are in your life at this point, it means different things to different people. For some, it's about believing in something—or someone—bigger than themselves. For others, as Larry has pointed out, it's as formal as organized religion. And to still others, it's less structured and more open to new influences in the world."

"Shouldn't there be a separation between our spiritual life and our work life?" Sydney inquired.

Since Miles had been through the training session at Halifax University, he knew the response Dennis had for this question. "Some people do everything they can to separate their spiritual life and their work life, and I'm convinced that's not possible. You see, there must be a connection between what we do, who we are, and what we value most in this life. For most people, what they *do* is their job—or career if they've found one—and who they *are* comes from their spirituality. Therefore, there must be a connection between our career and our faith. There are two things you can do to take control of your own satisfaction as it relates to *Spirituality*."

Dennis continued, "Somewhere deep inside you is your purpose. Some of you have found it, and others have not. You were put here to do something other than work a job you don't enjoy."

"I was put here to go fishing," Roger laughed.

No one laughed with Roger—not even his buddy Larry.

"Some people figure out their bigger purpose and make a living doing it," Sydney responded. "Some people think they are here to help others, and they go to work for a foundation that helps others. Some people experience the loss of a child to drugs and think they are here to help others cope, and they travel the country speaking to kids about staying away from drugs. I get that. But what about all the other work that has to be done. You can't tell me the clerk at the convenience store has been put here to do *that* job, or that a call center rep sitting in this room has been put here to handle calls."

Dennis contemplated his response. "It's important that you not confuse your vocation with your purpose. You're right that some people can find their purpose and earn a living pursuing it. Other people have a career and pursue their purpose outside of their job. They aren't always the same."

"So, how do we figure out our bigger purpose?" Deanna asked.

"As with everything else we've talked about, there are several ways. The one I'd like to share with you is this: Make time for contemplation. If you haven't identified your bigger purpose at this point in your life, you need to spend time figuring it out. It probably won't just land in your lap. You need to think about it. If you meditate, then spend some time meditating. If you pray, then spend some time praying. If you don't do any of those things, then just spend some time thinking about what matters most to you."

Miles was pushing toward another break. "One more lesson related to *Spirituality*."

Challenge Ten
Commit to a
cause greater
than yourself.

"Most people just live day-to-day for themselves," Dennis commented. "They get up in the morning, go to work, earn their money, go home, spend time with their families, and go to bed. They get up the next day and start the process all over again."

"Isn't that how it works?" Mattie asked.

"It's how it works for a lot of people," Dennis replied. "However, to develop the spiritual aspect of your life, you must commit to a cause greater than yourself."

"What does that look like?" Mattie asked.

"Well, it looks different to different people," Dennis responded. "For one person, it's about becoming a public servant because she doesn't like the way the government takes care of the people. For another, it's dedicating every free moment he has to an organization fighting cancer because he lost his wife to that horrible disease.

It's different for everyone. But ultimately, it's about making a commitment to a cause much greater than themselves. The specific action I would encourage each of you to take is this: Find your philanthropic passion. Determine what's important to you, and find a way to serve."

Dennis looked up at the clock and realized it was time for another break. "Okay, we've been sitting here a while, so let's take another break. You've now seen the model and the 10 challenges. When we get back from the break, you'll have a chance to discuss what you've learned in your groups. Be back in 15 minutes. I promise we'll start on time. Don't be late."

BREAK TIME

Larry and his new buddy headed outside with cigarettes in hand. Several team members headed for the snacks and drinks in the hallway. Miles and Sydney stayed at the table.

"Do you think this stuff makes a difference?" Sydney asked as he flipped through his notes.

"I know it does," Miles responded. "I've already been putting some of the ideas to work since the day I previewed the course at Halifax University. It's so simple it seems like we're wasting time talking about it. But, quite frankly, it's like everything else in life. If we don't do anything with the information, it won't matter. Like Dennis said at the beginning of the training, if we don't buy in to the ideas, it won't make any difference at all."

Sydney sat quietly for a moment. "You know, I learned something new today. I learned that I knew everything he presented, but I don't take steps to improve some of these areas of my life. I know I'm one of the engaged employees in our office, but I'm curious how making an improvement in some of these areas will enhance my life."

"I gained a lot from the simplicity of this training," Miles responded. "Perhaps the most significant thing I learned was that the key is not to make giant improvements in any of these areas. It's about making incremental improvements that can lead to significant changes in life satisfaction."

They sat quietly as Sydney thought about the incremental improvements he could make in his own life. He was happy, but he had no idea how much happier he would be.

THE CHALLENGE

About half the class members were in their seats after the 15-minute break. The other half hurried to their seats from the hallway when they realized Seth had arrived and was standing at the front of the class. "I hope you've enjoyed the class so far. I'm a big believer in training, but I realize that a real change in behavior comes from what happens when you leave the classroom. Dennis tells me that each of the groups will now be given time to apply some specific actions to the five areas he's introduced, and I think that's great. But I want to take it another step and issue a challenge."

All eyes were glued to Seth, including those of Larry and Roger. "Over the next five months, I challenge each group to add specific actions to the list you create today. Each month, the group you are with today will be given time to discuss a different aspect of the model. You'll be asked to submit some additional ideas. At the end of five months, we'll create our own sheet of actionable items created by you, the call center reps. The team with the best ideas will be awarded time off from work."

Seth fielded a few questions, and then Dennis got them started on their assignment. "At your table, I want you to discuss each of the five areas, then offer one specific action for each challenge we've introduced today. Whatever remaining time we have, you will be given a chance to put together your personal plan."

Miles loved a good challenge, and he welcomed this one with open arms.

A TIME TO CELEBRATE

Miles enjoyed the time he spent with the Dinner Club, but he was also becoming friends with his other team members. He remembered how aloof they had been at the very first team meeting, and he noticed they were finally starting to lighten up a little. Five months of good leadership can make a difference, Miles thought to himself.

As usual, Miles arrived early that morning and was sitting with a few of his fellow team members in the break room when Sydney walked in. "What am I missing this morning? If Miles is holding court, there must be something good happening."

"We're planning a celebration," Miles responded with a smile. "We've never done anything outside the office as a team, and we're making plans."

"What did you have in mind?"

"A barbeque cookout at my house," Miles beamed.

"At your house? There are 25 people on our team. Can you entertain that many people at one time?"

"Fifty people," Miles responded. "You're forgetting spouses. And yes, we can handle a group that big."

"Does Gabriela know about your grand plan to have 50 people take over her house?"

"Not yet," Miles smiled. "I plan to break the good news to her tonight. She loves planning these things."

Miles realized that even if he had to convince Gabriela his idea was a good one, it would be worth it to have the entire team together.

GET THE HOUSE READY

"You want to have *how* many people over for a cookout?" Gabriela asked with a shocked look on her face.

"Fifty, that's all," Miles responded as he unloaded the groceries from the trunk of the car. "Look, we spend a lot of time together at work, and I just thought it would be fun if we did something together outside the office."

"I think it's a great idea. I'm just trying to figure out how we're going to accommodate that many people. And, by the way, are you factoring in kids?"

"Yes," Miles responded. "Not all 25 people from our team will come. Some will be working the weekend shift, and some won't even understand why we're doing anything outside of the office. When you take those out and add in some kids, we'll be around 50. And I've arranged to borrow a barbeque pit big enough to cook all the food."

"All right, we'll figure out a way to make it work. I'm looking forward to meeting these people you talk about all the time. Maybe I can finally meet Larry."

"I would be surprised if Larry came to our house for a cookout," Miles responded. "If he does, maybe you can work on him a little. If he doesn't, we'll have fun anyway."

ELECTED SPOKESMAN

All four teams had gone through the life balance training in May, and, as Miles expected, the reaction was somewhat mixed. Although some people embraced the idea of bringing more satisfaction to their lives, others figured it was just another way for the company to get more from its employees.

Miles normally went home to see Gabriela before the Dinner Club met, but on this night he headed straight to La Cantina to review his notes from the training and prepare for their discussion. The group was energized by Seth's challenge at the training session, and they'd agreed to use their time at Dinner Club to brainstorm their ideas.

"I win the bet," Mattie laughed as she walked toward the table with Sydney and Deanna close behind.

"What bet?" Miles asked.

"Deanna and Sydney said you'd be running late tonight, but I told them you'd be here early with your notes out and ready to go when we got here."

"What did you win?" Miles asked with a smile.

"Let's just say I'll be ordering the most expensive thing on the menu tonight."

"Well, good for you," Miles replied. "That'll teach the two of you to underestimate me!"

"Hey, where is Mr. Doom-and-Gloom?" Deanna asked as she sat down.

"I don't know," Sydney replied. "He called in sick today, so I guess he won't be here."

Mattie started to laugh out loud. "Does negativity count as a sickness?"

Everyone laughed at her question, except Miles. "I have a question. How did Larry ever get invited to be a part of this group? He is so unlike anyone here. He drags down every conversation we have."

"He invited himself," Sydney responded. "We were sitting in the break room discussing our first Dinner Club, and he overheard our conversation. He just showed up, and no one had the nerve to tell him he wasn't invited."

"Am I the only one who thinks we would enjoy our time together a lot more if he wasn't a part of this group?" Miles asked.

Deanna was normally the quiet one in the group, and certainly the one who would be the least likely to say anything bad about Larry. "I get tired of his negativity sometimes, but I guess I just hoped being around positive people might change him. I was hoping we might rub off on him."

"That's a great objective," Miles responded, "but do you think it's working? How long have you been meeting?"

"We started the same month I got here," Deanna answered. "November of last year."

"This is June. With the exception of this month and the month we took off, he has been coming to Dinner Club for six months. Does he seem any more positive now than he was in the beginning?"

Sydney thought about the question for a moment. "Not really. In fact, in some ways he's gotten even worse."

"What's his deal?" Mattie asked.

"I don't know," Sydney responded. "I've worked with him for years, and he's always been the same way. I didn't want him to join our group, but I didn't know how to tell him he wasn't invited."

"Maybe we should just start meeting somewhere else?" Mattie laughed. "We don't have to tell him, do we?"

"I love getting together once a month with all of you," Miles stated. "But quite frankly, I don't enjoy it knowing Larry will be here. I'm reading a book

right now that examines the things highly successful people do to be highly successful. One of the
things it notes is that highly successful people
refuse to be around people who bring them down.
Larry brings me down every time I'm around him."

"Have you told him that?" Deanna asked.

"No, but I've pointed out his negativity. Maybe
I should just tell him he needs to keep his negativity to himself or stop coming to our Dinner Club."

"We elect you as our spokesman," Mattie
smiled.

"Does everyone agree that he needs to cheer
up or find another group to hang out with?"

Every head around the table nodded in agreement. Miles was never a fan of being the bearer
of bad news, but it was time for Larry to make a
change. "I'll deal with him later. In the meantime,
what did everybody think of the training?"

"I liked it," Sydney responded. "In some ways
I thought it was too simple, but when I asked
myself if I was actually doing those things, I realized I wasn't."

"I agree," Mattie added, "and I need some more
practical ideas to implement. I'm hoping Seth's
challenge will get everyone on our team thinking
of more ways to implement the ideas."

"How about we win this little challenge?" Miles
said, grinning. "Let's get started with *Career*. What
did everyone think about the trainer's observation
about a job versus a career?"

Mattie offered the first comment. "I thought
it was exactly right. In fact, I think it's part of

the problem we have in our office. Most people don't give much thought to their career. They start working somewhere and it's a job, and then they get comfortable when they feel secure. They stay for the security, not because it's a passion. Ten years later, they still see it as a job, and they continue to drag themselves to work every day."

"So, the first challenge is to ask the hard questions about our careers," Miles continued as he read his notes. "The question given in the training was, 'Are you giving it your all?' What other questions do you think we should be asking that could enhance this aspect of life?"

"I have one," Deanna interjected. "When people complain about their job, they always seem to follow it up with the fact they're looking for another job. I saw a study that showed the majority of people *are* looking for another job. I'm curious why they think it would be different anyplace else. In other words, if they're disengaged where they are, what makes them think they wouldn't just take their disengagement with them? Here's my question: Would a different job matter?"

"Nice," Miles smiled. "Does everyone agree that should be our question?"

He looked around the table and everyone nodded in agreement. "Okay, let's move on to the second challenge related to *Career:* Focus on your own personal growth. The specific action from the training was to pursue training offered by the company. That one seems so obvious to me, but apparently there are a lot of people who take it for granted. Any thoughts on another specific action for this one?"

"I'm taking an online course right now to learn to speak Spanish," Deanna said. "I get some customers who call in speaking Spanish, and I can't help them."

"That's why we have Spanish-speaking reps available to handle those calls during each shift," Sydney replied.

"I know, but I *want* to be able to speak Spanish. I figure it's a skill I can take with me to any job, and I might need it in my personal life, as well. I found the course online, and I can do it at my own pace."

"Does everyone agree that taking online classes should be our specific action for focus on our own personal growth?" Miles asked.

Everyone nodded in agreement. "Okay, so we've completed our first assignment. I'll give our ideas to Seth, and we'll see how we do."

Miles was putting his notes away when Deanna spoke up. "By the way, Seth authorized my day off even though I haven't completed six months."

"I told you he would work with you," Mattie replied.

"And you were right about Carmen, too. I was on a shift when I saw the fight between Seth and Carmen in his office. Apparently she was mad that he gave me the time off."

"It's nice to know he didn't just cave in," Sydney replied. "And it's nice to know we have a boss who will fight for us."

"Speaking of fighting," Mattie interrupted. "I get angry when I'm hungry, and I'm getting very hungry. Let's order!"

FIRE UP THE GRILL

Miles loved to cook barbeque, and he was excited to cook for such a large group of people. He had just returned from a weeklong family vacation to Disneyland, and he had a lot to do to get ready. He asked Sydney to come over early that morning to start getting everything ready for the cookout in the afternoon.

"I've never seen a barbeque pit with wheels on it," Sydney laughed as he walked up the driveway. "Where did you get that thing?"

"Nice, isn't it?" Miles smiled. "A friend of mine brought it down from Dallas. He cooks in those barbeque competitions and takes it around to cook for charity events and church outings. We could cook for the entire neighborhood on this thing."

Sydney walked over, opened the lid, and saw that food was already on the pit and cooking. "When did you start cooking?"

"Around midnight last night. My friend said the trick to cooking on this big pit is 'low and slow.' I've been cooking some of the stuff since midnight. We'll get the rest of it done this morning, and it should all be ready by the time everyone gets here this afternoon."

That afternoon was one of the best times Miles had with a group of employees in his

20 years with Halifax. The majority of the team showed up with spouses and children, as did Seth. Gabriela had rented a Moon Bounce for the younger kids, and it was filled the entire day. The older kids played video games all afternoon. Miles served up smoked brisket, ribs, chicken, and sausage. It was a warm June day, and everyone had a great time. Too bad Larry chose to not make an appearance.

REFLECTION

"That was fun," Gabriela said as she was putting dishes in the dishwasher. "I think everyone had a good time."

"Yeah, I agree. It was nice to do something outside of the office. I learned some things about people I didn't know before. I think it will make a difference for our team."

"Do you think Seth had a good time?" she asked.

"I do. I figured he would stop by for a while and leave, but he stayed the whole time. That's a pretty good sign he enjoyed himself."

Miles and Gabriela had been on their feet the entire day. They finished the dishes and then headed to the backyard to sit in a swing and relax. Miles shared his thoughts about how he believed the training would help everyone in the office find more satisfaction in their lives. As he looked back, he realized that it was already working in his.

GAINING ATTENTION

It was the beginning of the third quarter, so Miles figured the managers would be having another quarterly meeting to discuss the *Engaged Leadership* program. Miles enjoyed the weeks following the quarterly meetings because he always knew Seth would be practicing what he learned from Hannah.

When Seth called a last-minute team meeting with the team members on duty that Monday morning, he figured Hannah must have shared some good news. He was right.

"As you all know," Seth began, "the management team has been working hard to try to create a culture of employee engagement. We truly want this office to be a place you come because you want to be here, not just a place you have to come to do a job. Although Hannah can teach the lessons and the managers can implement the ideas, it takes an office full of call center reps who will respond with good results."

"Good leadership makes a difference," offered one of the team members at the end of the conference table.

"Well, I appreciate that. I'm not sure whether it's good leadership, good ideas from the Engagement Team, or the fact everyone is focusing on the training we did in May, but our results are improving, and I appreciate it. In fact, they're improving so much we've gotten the attention of our corporate headquarters. Hannah's boss told his boss about the improvements we've made, and she's planning a visit. She'll be here in a few weeks. Our team has experienced the most improvement, so I've been asked to make one of the presentations. I may be calling on some of you to help."

"Let us know how we can help," Miles replied.

"I will. In the meantime, everyone go out and enjoy a safe celebration for the Fourth of July. I understand Aaron brought a cake and put it in the break room. Somebody have a piece for me."

FORE!

"I have a feeling I'll be spending more time today looking for my golf ball," Sydney announced as he got out of the cart and headed into the brush.

"I'm not sure I'll do much better," Miles responded as he dug in his bag to get another ball. "Someone once said the key to a balanced life is finding a hobby. I'm not sure this hobby brings me any balance at all. In fact, I seem to be more stressed when I'm done playing 18 holes than when I started."

Miles enjoyed being around Sydney. Not only did he look forward to going to work because he enjoyed being around him, he enjoyed spending time with him outside of work. Sydney had become more than a coworker. He was a friend, and Miles liked to spend time with his friends.

The two of them had taken that Tuesday off from work to play a round of golf. Saturday was reserved for Gabriela and the boys, and Sunday was reserved for church and relaxation. It was a hot July day in central Texas, but it was an easy choice for Miles to take the day off during the week to spend it with his friend.

Miles and Sydney enjoyed competition, and they each fought hard to beat the other in this round of golf. However, neither of them played the game very often, so the fact they were competing was rather comical. At some point they stopped keeping score and just enjoyed the day.

After they finished the eighteenth hole, Miles parked the cart and they walked into the Capitol Grill, the restaurant located at the golf course. After they sat down, Sydney said, "I'm starving. What are you having today?"

"A burger sounds good, but I think I'm going with that soup-and-sandwich combo thing. I've been trying to eat a little better."

"Gabriela has you on some fancy diet, doesn't she?" Sydney laughed. "You are half my size. Why are you worried about weight?"

"First of all, Gabriela doesn't have me on a diet. Second, I'm just trying to focus on my health a little more."

"Are you going to become one of those health nuts, counting every calorie you put in your mouth now that you've been through that training?" Sydney asked.

"Not at all, although I don't think watching your calories is such a bad thing. I'm just trying to make some better choices when I can, and this is one of those times."

"Before you know it you'll be hanging out in the gym every morning before work," Sydney laughed as he reached for his glass of water.

"Now that you mention it, I was going to suggest we start hitting the treadmill in the morning. Halifax has that gym downstairs from the office. We can meet up early on the mornings we're working the same shift."

Sydney hadn't missed many meals in his life. "Okay, I'll give it a try. But for now, I'm eating that burger. I'll run tomorrow."

GUT INSTINCT

"Did you win?" Gabriela asked when she heard the front door close.

"Golf is not always about who wins and who loses," Miles answered as he walked into the kitchen.

"That usually means you lost," Gabriela laughed. "How bad?"

"No idea. We gave up keeping score about halfway through. It turns out golf isn't all that bad when you stop keeping score and just have fun."

"Well, I'm glad you and Sydney got to spend some time together," Gabriela responded. "It's always nice to have people at work you like being around."

Miles realized he hadn't shared with Gabriela his dilemma about Larry Marcus. "Speaking of people at work, that reminds me of someone I *don't* like being around."

"You must be talking about Larry."

"He's the one," Miles responded shaking his head. "He just destroys the energy at our Dinner Club, and he refuses to take any responsibility for his own happiness."

"Abraham Lincoln once said that most people are about as happy as they make up their minds to be. I suppose some people prefer not to take responsibility for their own happiness. They can't blame themselves if things don't get better in their world."

"When did you start quoting dead presidents?" Miles laughed.

"It's just one of those quotes that always stuck in my mind. And by the way, there is some value in having negative people around, Miles. Before you try anything new, they'll usually tell you what will go wrong because they always look for the bad stuff. You may not want to run him off."

"That makes sense, but he just drains us of any energy we have, and I've been elected to tell him he's got to change his outlook or change his plans the first Friday of every month."

"What does your gut instinct tell you?"

"My gut tells me he can't change," Miles responded. "I honestly hope I'm wrong, but my gut tells me he can't change."

"Follow your gut instinct. I have never met anyone who has a more accurate gut instinct than you. Follow your gut."

A DIFFICULT CONVERSATION

Miles was not looking forward to the conversation he planned to have with Larry regarding his negativity, but he had promised his friends he would have it, and he intended to keep his promise. The time never seemed to be right. As he pulled into the Halifax parking lot and saw Larry standing next to his car, he thought the timing might never get better.

As Miles walked toward Larry, he noticed how the natural sunlight made the frown lines in Larry's face stand out. For the first time, Miles could literally see the bitterness in Larry's face.

"I didn't know you were a smoker," Miles commented to Larry as he got out of his car.

Larry gave his trademark glare-over-the-glasses look. "There's a lot you don't know about me, Miles."

"Anything you care to share?"

"Anything in particular you'd like to know?" Larry asked as he leaned against his car.

"I noticed you didn't make it to the cookout. Was the thought of eating my food too much for you to handle?"

"I spend all week with you people," Larry responded as he took a long drag of his cigarette. "I'm not about to spend the weekend with you, too."

"Larry, you've been here a long time. You have more skill and knowledge than most call center reps will ever gain, yet all of that is overshadowed by your intense negativity. What's that about?"

"Maybe you're the only one who thinks I have this intense negativity," Larry responded as he shifted nervously.

"No, I don't think I am, Larry. Everyone in our Dinner Club sees it, and quite frankly, it's wearing us out. Is there anything we can do to help you see that not everything is as bad as you make it out to be?"

Larry tossed his cigarette butt on the ground and stepped on it with the toe of his shoe. "First of all, mind your own business. I see things as I want to see them. And second, if everyone in our little group thinks my negativity is too intense for them, then maybe I'll just stop going. It's a stupid little group anyway."

Miles watched as Larry walked across the parking lot and into the building. He started this conversation thinking he was "firing" Larry from the group, and it turned out he quit way before he could be fired.

A SIGH OF RELIEF

All eyes were on Miles as he walked into La Cantina. It had been only a day since he'd had his conversation with Larry, but he hadn't told anyone of the outcome.

Sydney broke the silence. "Well, did you talk to Larry?"

"I did," Miles responded as he pulled out a chair and sat down. "He quit."

"He quit his job?" Mattie responded with a shocked look.

"No, he quit our group."

"He quit our group?" It was Mattie again. "He can't quit our group. He wasn't even invited to be a part of it in the first place. He's the one with the problem, and he thinks he can just walk away and . . ."

Miles held up his hand and interrupted Mattie before she could finish her comment. "Relax. It needed to be his choice. I talked with Larry to tell him our concerns about his negativity, and to let him know he needed to change or he couldn't be a part of our group anymore. Before I could, he said he would quit coming."

"Was he mad?" Sydney asked.

"No, he wasn't mad. I just have this feeling something is going on with him that none of us knows about. I wish we could figure it out so maybe we could help him get past all the bitterness that seems to be going on inside him."

"He has to want to share it before we can help him," Sydney responded.

"True," agreed Miles. "Hey, are you guys ready to talk about the next section?"

Miles took out his notes and flipped to the page titled "Relationships." He took a sip from his glass and said, "The first challenge was to surround ourselves with the right people, and I thought Dennis hit the nail on the head. The people we surround ourselves with have so much impact on our lives. Gabriela and I spend a lot of time with the boys, making sure they are hanging out with the right kinds of friends. We all know as parents how influential friends can be, but we seldom consider it for ourselves. I think it's very important."

"The specific action the trainer provided was to analyze our crew, ensuring we have people around us who support us. What's another specific thing we can do to surround ourselves with the right people?" Sydney asked.

"I think we've already done something related to that," Miles answered. "We filtered Larry and his negativity out of the group. We made an effort to try to help him, and when he wasn't willing to accept any help, we separated ourselves from the negative impact he could have on our group. So that's my suggestion: Filter the negativity."

"I like it," Sydney responded nodding his head. "Anyone disagree that filtering the negativity should be our specific action."

When no one disagreed, Miles moved them along as he read from his notes. "The next challenge is enhancing work relationships. The suggestion given in the class was to do what you say you're going to do. Does anyone have another specific action?"

The group was quiet for a moment before Mattie broke the silence. "I think we should lift each other up. You know, Seth does a great job of motivating our group, but he's not always around, nor does he always see what we do. We can either sit around and hope he sees what we're accomplishing, or we can recognize each other when we accomplish stuff at work. For me, if my fellow team members are lifting me up, that's enhancing the relationship I have with them."

"Well said," Miles responded. "Anyone have a problem with that being our specific action?"

Miles looked around the table. "If no one is in disagreement, then let's order something to eat. I will tell Seth about our suggestions."

"I can't stay," Mattie said as she grabbed her purse. "Seth promised to buy dinner for my husband and me if I reached six months with perfect attendance. He gave me a gift certificate, so I'm surprising my husband with dinner tonight."

As Mattie left, Miles was impressed that Seth remembered his promise. He was even more impressed that he kept his word.

A VISIT FROM THE BIG BOSS

Miles knew the executive from corporate headquarters was coming, but he didn't realize it was that day. He was sitting at a computer station early that morning when he saw Hannah walk through the office with a visitor. Miles was handling a call when the two ladies walked by, so Hannah nodded her head and mouthed "Good morning" as they walked past.

Miles was just returning to his computer station after his morning break when Hannah approached him and asked him to come into her office. After the two walked into her office, Hannah closed the door and said, "Miles, I'd like you to meet Amanda Suttle."

"Good morning," Miles smiled as he extended his hand. "It's nice to meet you, ma'am."

"You Texas men and your manners," Amanda said as she shook her head. "I already had to explain to Seth on the ride from the airport to call me Amanda."

"Sorry, Amanda. I was born and raised in Texas, and my mother . . ."

Amanda raised her hand and interrupted Miles before he could go any further. "I know, I know. Your mother taught you it's a sign of respect. Had the same conversation with Seth earlier this morning, and I appreciate the kindness."

Everyone settled into a chair before Hannah started. "Amanda heard about the success we've enjoyed here at our call center. She's come down from New Jersey for the day and will be spending the afternoon with the managers. They'll be presenting her with what they've done and how they think it's made a difference in the office. But I think it's important she hear from the people on the front line."

"That's right, Miles," Amanda interjected. "I'm looking forward to hearing what the managers have to say. In fact, I bet they've been working on presentations since the moment they heard I was coming for a visit. They've had a chance to think about everything and plan out their message. You haven't; however, I want to know what's making a difference in this office, and I want to hear it from you."

Miles sat quietly for just a moment. "Wow. The managers got two and a half weeks to prepare and I get two and a half seconds. Quite frankly, there isn't much need to prepare, I've worked for Halifax for 20 years, and I've experienced good and bad leaders. There isn't much surprise that the performance of the office is always tied to the quality of the leadership. I don't know what Hannah has been teaching the managers, but whatever it is must be working."

"What are you seeing from the leaders?" Amanda asked as she leaned forward in her chair.

"The sharing of information. Flexibility with individual needs. A commitment to education and recognition of accomplishments."

"Give me some specifics," Amanda directed.

"Sure. They let people know where they stand. All employees want to be satisfied, and satisfaction usually comes from accomplishing something. They put up these scoreboards to serve as a reminder of how close we are to our objectives. Some people like them and some don't, but it's hard to argue with results. The employees in this office are more engaged, and the results are improving."

"Tell me about this life balance training everyone attended a few months ago."

"Overall, it was a mixed reaction. For those who embraced the message, it was great. For those who were cynical, it was just another program. But here's what it did. It gave the employees the information and tools they needed to make a difference in their personal lives. The program showed how it all ties together, and that when we're more engaged in our personal lives, we give ourselves the chance to become engaged at work."

"How long did you say you've been at Halifax?" Amanda asked.

"Twenty years."

"Why aren't you a manager?" Amanda asked as she looked toward Hannah.

"I spent some time as an interim manager in another call center. I've had a few chances during my career, but the timing was never right in my personal life. Besides, I enjoy being a call center rep."

"Well, if that ever changes, you let me know."

IT'S ALL GOOD

Miles was looking forward to getting home to tell Gabriela about his experience with Amanda Suttle. In fact, he hoped to tell the entire family about his experience. He was reminded quickly how little interest 12-year-old twins have in their father's career, and how hanging out with their friends the moment they finished eating was much more important.

He did, however, get to share his experience with Gabriela. For the rest of the evening, he talked about how well things were going at work. They talked about how well the kids had settled into a new town. They talked about how good their church life was. They were very happy where they were in life. For a brief moment, Miles wasn't sure anything could upset his perfectly balanced life at this point. Unfortunately, life has a way of changing just as we think everything is right in the world.

CALL HOME

Miles struggled with the idea of texting someone when he could pick up the same telephone and call that person. He was turning 42 years old in a few weeks, and he didn't want to be the old fuddy-duddy who refused to go along with technology. Gabriela knew his hang-up with texting, so she seldom sent him a text message, and never when he was working.

When he received her simple text message that read "Call home," he knew something was wrong. It wasn't the message that led him to that conclusion. It was the time of day. Miles hadn't ended his shift for the day.

After Miles called home and spoke with Gabriela, the shift coordinator notified Seth that Miles would be gone for the rest of the day. By the time he got home, Gabriela had already packed a bag and was ready to drive him to the airport. For the next few hours, Miles would have a chance to allow the news to sink in. He had friends who had been through this struggle, but he never had. He needed those friends now. He needed someone to help him deal with the fact that his father was diagnosed with stage IV colon cancer.

A SLIP IN THE POLLS

Miles spent a week at his parents' house in San Diego. They had moved to California when they retired so they could be in a temperate climate. Miles had suggested Florida, but Seth's father refused to hang out with a bunch of "old people" and his mother wanted to avoid the hurricanes.

During his visit, Miles had the opportunity to work through a plan of action for his father. Miles had always been the strong one in the family, and they needed him to put it all in perspective.

Miles enjoyed the cooler temperatures in San Diego, but he was ready to get back into his routine when he returned to Texas. As he walked into the break room, he saw Deanna sitting at a table by herself reading a book. "That doesn't look like a Tom Clancy novel to me. What are you reading?"

Deanna slowly looked up from her book, and then leaped to her feet when she saw it was Miles. "You're back! We've been worried sick about you. How is your dad?"

"He's fine. I'll tell you all about it later. What did I miss while I was gone?"

"Well, after holding our own in June and July, we had a little slip in the polls," Deanna said. "We moved from first place in attendance to second, but other than that everything is the same."

"What is that book you're reading?

Deanna flipped over to the front cover. "It's a book about financial planning. I figure no one is going to come along to teach me about financial planning, so I'm trying to figure it out on my own. This is the first time I've had a job where I've made any real money, and I want to learn the right way to manage it early in my life."

"Sounds like you're focusing on your own personal growth," Miles smiled. "Maybe you can teach us all a few things when you're done."

Miles got his coffee, and they spent some time talking about California. For Miles, it was good to be home.

REAL FRIENDS

Miles had grown to appreciate the friendships he had established with his fellow team members in the Dinner Club. He knew they were friends, but he didn't realize how much they meant to him until he saw how supportive they were regarding the news of his father. For the first half hour at the Dinner Club on that Friday evening in August, they poured out their love and support as he shared with them all the details about his father's situation.

"I suppose there is a little irony in the fact we're talking about this next topic tonight, *Health*," Miles laughed as he took out his notes. "But let's get started so we can just hang out this evening. The first challenge is to focus on our physical health. The suggestion from the class was to learn about nutrition and practice it. That was probably the biggest 'duh' moment of the training for me, but I wonder how many people made a single change after the training was over."

"It got my attention," Sydney admitted. "I'm not counting calories, but I'm at least trying to make some better choices. My life isn't any slower now, so I still don't have time to cook nutritious meals every night, but I'm making better choices. I've been searching online and finding nutritional information, and I got an application for my cell phone that provides nutritional information, as well."

"Good," Miles responded and then turned to Mattie and Deanna. "And by the way, Sydney and

I work out in the mornings a few days a week in the Halifax gym if either of you ever want to join us. Also, if you haven't seen the posters in the office, there is a Halloween marathon coming up in October. We may have to walk most of it, but we're training for it. Feel free to join us."

Miles turned back to his notes. "All right, who has a suggestion for a second specific action related to physical health?"

"How about getting proper rest?" Deanna offered. "Our modern-day culture has everyone running a million miles an hour. Kids are more involved than ever; both parents are working more hours than ever; and everybody seems to be struggling to get everything done. I took a class in college that addressed the whole issue of sleep deprivation. We talked about how people seem to think they have trained their bodies to operate on less sleep, but that it doesn't work that way. As a result, performance on the job suffers because we're physically tired from a lack of sleep."

"I like that," Miles responded. "Let's make that our specific action. How about emotional health? The suggestion given in class was to keep it all in perspective. Any thoughts on an additional action?"

"Dennis mentioned that our emotional health is shaped by our experiences," Sydney offered. "Sometimes those experiences are good, and sometimes they are very hurtful. Perhaps one of the best ways to enhance our emotional health is to let go of some of those hurtful things. When my wife left me a few years ago, I was very angry.

To this day, I'm still carrying around that bitterness like an anchor. I'm sure that is affecting my emotional health."

"I'm sure you're not alone," Mattie answered. "I have several of my own anchors."

"Cut loose the anchors," Miles responded. "That will be our specific action.

"Good," Sydney replied. "I'm hungry. I can accept the irony that we're at a Mexican food restaurant talking about health, but I don't think we need to change our location. Maybe we can just alter our selections every now and then. I challenge everyone to order something healthier than you did last month."

Miles smiled at the suggestion. He knew changes in behavior always started with the smallest of steps.

BATTER UP

Miles grew up playing sports. He had played football as a child, so he knew the dangers that came with getting knocked around. Although he was happy his twins chose to play baseball instead of football, he never looked forward to the summer heat and humidity of Texas while he sat in the stands watching them play.

He loved watching his sons play baseball, and he liked that Sydney's son played in the same league. They were playing each other that evening, so Miles knew it would be a fun night of baseball.

"So, how are things?" Sydney asked as they watched the teams warm up on the field.

Miles knew what he was talking about. "As good as can be expected, I guess. We're coping, and we're learning as much as we can about the alternatives. How about you?"

"Nothing in my life is as stressful as dealing with a parent with cancer."

"Maybe not," Miles responded, "but we all have our issues."

"True. I guess overall things are pretty good, particularly when I keep it all in perspective. I've been dealing with this divorce for a couple years now, and I'm telling you, I can't seem to let go of all this anger. Divorce is bad enough, but when some-one just walks away . . ."

Miles could see the pain on Sydney's face for the first time. "At least you have custody of your son."

"You got that right, brother," Sydney said as he started to smile again. "I've never worked so hard in my life. Trying to work a job and raising my son, it's hard work. I've prayed more over the past year than I did my entire life. I'm not sure if it's helped, but overall, life has been good."

"You seem to be enjoying work."

"Yeah, I have," Sydney replied. "I'll be honest, if I couldn't look forward to seeing you every day and hanging out with our Dinner Club group, I wouldn't enjoy it as much. And don't get me wrong, I still don't bounce out of bed and head to work every morning. But I've finally figured out a way to weave all these pieces together, and it's made a difference in the way I see my job."

"Before long," Miles smiled, "you'll meet someone new and settle down again."

"I just hope I can find a perfect relationship like the one you have with Gabriela."

"Perfect relationship? Is that what you think? Our relationship is far from perfect. Like every parent, we have trouble with the kids. And with us, it's times two. I want to be the best employee I can be, but what I really want is to be the best husband and father I can be. I recognize now that it all ties together."

"Well," Sydney laughed, "whatever it is, that's what I hope to have some day."

Miles hoped the same for his friend.

MUY BIEN

Miles was very competitive, whether the challenges were sports-related or work-related. The competition between teams in the office motivated him to work hard, and it also inspired him to push his fellow team members.

"Have you noticed there is one category in which our team cannot get to first place?" Miles asked the group as they sat down at La Cantina.

"First Resolution Rate," Sydney replied. "We come close every month, and we're now in second place, but we can't seem to get to first place."

"Does anyone know whose name is at the bottom of the list in the office?" Miles asked.

"Not just the bottom of *our* team's list, but the bottom of the list for the entire office."

"Larry Marcus," Mattie replied.

"That's right," Miles responded, "and what's that about? The guy has been around 14 years, and he's the worst in the office. It's not difficult. It's the percentage of calls completed with a single contact. Why doesn't he just handle his own stuff instead of transferring the calls to other people?"

"I don't know," Deanna answered, "but we may start to see some changes. I overheard Larry telling someone in the break room that Seth has had a few conversations with him about it. Apparently, Seth is a little upset about not being able to get to first place as well."

"Enough of Larry," Sydney remarked. "I get wound up every time we bring up his name."

"Fair enough," Miles responded as he pulled out his notes. "Let's move along to *Finances*, which Dennis called the most taboo of all aspects."

Sydney joined in. "It's also the one he said impacts so many of the other areas. A struggle with finances impacts your career, relationships, health, and spirituality."

"Let's see here," Miles continued as he read his notes. "The first challenge is to tie our financials to our bigger goals. The specific action shared in the training was to stop comparing ourselves to others. Who has a suggestion for another action?"

Deanna spoke up first. "I've been thinking about this one, and this answer may be the most obvious, but I think people need to learn to manage their money. I'm just getting started, but it seems most people don't know how to manage their money, based on how many people are struggling."

"I agree," Mattie said. "Let's go with that one for our suggestion. Also, here comes the waiter, and I'm starving. Let's order dinner so we can eat by the time we finish the second point."

The waiter walked up to the table to take their orders. Before anyone could order, Deanna spoke up first. *"¿Por favor, puedo tener el plato de enchiladas y un margarita?"*

Everyone stopped reading the menu and looked over at Deanna as she closed her menu. The waiter looked over and said, *"Sí, señora. ¿Quieres guacamole en el lado?"*

"No, gracias, pero quiero una taza de té también."

"Well, just look at you carrying on a conversation in Spanish," Sydney smiled.

"I'm at the advanced level of my online course."

"Have you tried to talk to any customers in the call center yet?" Mattie asked.

"No. I'll just stick with the easy stuff here."

"Well, since you are the only one at the table who can carry on a conversation in Spanish, perhaps we can get back to our conversation in a language we can all speak," Miles laughed.

"¡No problema!"

After everyone had ordered, Miles continued the discussion. "The next challenge is adding more value to our employer. The suggestion in class was to find ways to make or save the company money. Any thoughts on another suggestion?"

Sydney responded first. "Yeah, I've been thinking about this one, and I'd suggest we become solution finders. Anyone can find problems and take them to a manager. The solutions we offer may not make or save the company any money, but we're certainly adding value by bringing solutions to the table instead of problems."

"I like it," Sydney replied. "I think we just got our two suggestions for the night. Now, put your notes away and let's relax."

MOVIE TIME

Miles was determined to spend more time with Gabriela, so they started a monthly date night. They preferred a weekly date night, but that seemed to push the limits while raising two kids. A new movie had just been released, and they were in the car headed to the theater for that month's date night.

"We haven't had a chance to talk much about work since you came back from San Diego," Gabriela started. "Anything new?"

"Not much. I did run into one of Carmen's employees in the gym the other morning. She heard about our cookout and didn't understand why the company didn't do things for their team. I had to explain to her that the company didn't do the cookout—our team coordinated that on our own."

"Was she surprised?"

"Yeah, she was surprised," Miles responded. "She was surprised that we did it on our own, but she was almost confused that we care so much about improving our team, since they aren't paying us more money."

"For some people it's all about the money."

"Yes it is," Miles nodded as he turned into the parking lot of the movie theater.

"And how is Deanna? We had the nicest conversation at the cookout a few months ago. She seems like such a nice young lady."

"Deanna is doing great. She started out pretty disengaged, but she's one on our team who has really responded to the engaged culture. It's been fun watching her progress, since she's only been around a few months. In fact, I made an interesting observation about her the other day."

"And what was that?"

"Deanna loves to read," Miles answered as they got out of the car. "She goes to a table by herself on her breaks, and if there isn't an empty table, she goes outside. Many of the other employees—particularly those from Carmen's team—use their break as an opportunity to gather together to complain. Deanna never joins those groups. Instead, she uses her breaks to do something she enjoys. Not exactly sure what that means, but I thought it was an interesting observation."

With that, work talk was over, and date night was under way.

THE RUMOR MILL

Miles was just pulling into the parking lot at Halifax when he got the text message from Mattie: GOT SOME NEWS!!!!!!

Miles wasn't sure he had ever received a text message from Mattie that didn't have all capital letters and multiple exclamation points. When he walked into the break room, he saw Mattie and Sydney sitting at a table by themselves, so he walked over and pulled up a chair.

"So, what's the news?" he asked.

"Shhh. No one knows about this one."

"First of all," Miles whispered as he looked around the break room. "We're the only ones in here, so I don't think we need to whisper. Second, if it's that good, I'm going to need a cup of coffee before you get started."

After Miles returned with his coffee in hand, Mattie leaned forward and shared her news. "Rumor has it that Jill is getting canned."

"Canned? You mean like fired?"

"Don't know," she whispered. "Apparently it's about to happen, so be prepared."

"Well, it doesn't affect me, so I'm not all that excited about your news, Mrs. Brown. And I know how inaccurate the rumor mill can be, so I'll believe it when I hear it from a legitimate source."

Sydney laughed at his disinterest in her story. "By the way, Miles and I are running in the Halloween marathon in two weeks. Are you joining us?"

"Probably not," Mattie smiled as she looked down at her watch. "And speaking of running, we have a shift starting in three minutes."

Mattie and Sydney headed into the call center to start their shifts. Miles had another half hour to enjoy his coffee, so he flipped through the channels on the television until he found his favorite show. Miles just loved reruns of *The Golden Girls*.

A HIGHER POWER

"You're here early," Miles said to Mattie as he wandered into La Cantina. "Don't you usually pick up your kids on Friday?"

"Yeah, that's usually the plan, but my husband picked them up today. He lost his job this week, so he's taking care of kid duty."

"I'm sorry to hear it," Miles responded. "Is everything working out okay?"

"You know me. I worry about everything. Even though we knew it was coming, I'm still worried about him finding another job."

Miles continued to calm Mattie's concerns while they waited for the others to arrive. Once they were all there, Miles got them started. "Don't forget, we're not meeting next month for Dinner Club. I'm taking Gabriela and the boys to California to see my dad, so I'll be on vacation all week. Sydney can't make it either. We'll have an extra-special gathering in December when we're all back in town."

Deanna looked up with a sad look on her face. "Great. I finally have a reason to celebrate and everybody leaves town."

"What are you celebrating?" Sydney asked.

"My one-year anniversary at Halifax. I started last November. I guess we'll just celebrate in December when everyone is back in town."

"Who says we have to wait?" Miles smiled. "We're all here right now. We'll raise a glass and celebrate tonight, and we'll celebrate again in December."

After they got the attention of the waitress and put in their order, Miles got the group started as he opened up his notes. "Let's jump in to the final aspect, *Spirituality*. The first challenge was about figuring out our bigger purpose, and the suggested action was to make time for contemplation. Any thoughts on a second action?"

When no one offered a suggestion, Miles provided his input. "I know how I go about finding my bigger purpose, and it ties in to the suggestion we got in class to make time for contemplation. Some people may meditate and others may just stare out a window, but my method of contemplation is prayer. I have my religious beliefs, and I appreciate the fact that not everyone will share mine. However, I think it's important that everyone believe in something, so my suggestion is this: Depend on a higher power. I depend on a higher power every day, and I'm happy to talk to anyone about those beliefs. But regardless of people's beliefs, I think they should depend on a higher power—whatever that may be for them. Anyone disagree with that being our suggestion?"

"I absolutely agree that it should be our suggestion," Sydney responded. "It's not pushing a belief onto anyone else. It's just suggesting that everyone should believe in—and depend on—a higher power."

"Good," Miles responded, "then let's take a look at the last challenge, committing to a cause greater than yourself. The specific action given in the class was to find your philanthropic passion. Any suggestions on another action?"

Mattie responded this time. "I've been giving this a lot of thought since the training. My husband and I never committed ourselves to anything other than raising our children. They are still our number one priority, but we've spent a lot of time talking about how much we're giving back. A few years ago, my husband lost his grandmother to Alzheimer's disease, and it was a painful thing for him and his family to experience. We never did much to commit to helping because we never had the money to donate. However, we've realized we can give a lot more than just money. Based on that, I'd like to suggest we offer the following action: Commit your time, talent, and treasure. There may be a day we can afford to write a check, but in the meantime, we can offer our time and talent. I've been volunteering my time after work, and my husband has been helping with the computers in this organization's office, since that's the skill he has. It's allowed us to commit to a cause greater than ourselves when we didn't even think it was possible."

Miles waited a moment to see whether anyone responded. "Wow. That may be the best one so far. I think that definitely should be our additional action."

"Hey, Mattie," Deanna said. "I'd like to offer to help you sometime if you need some help. My grandfather has Alzheimer's. I've never talked about it, but maybe that would be a way I could give back."

"If you're willing to help, I'll definitely get you the information. There are plenty of ways to help."

With that, Miles wrapped up the conversation. "Okay, we're finished. Time to eat!"

GIVING THANKS

Miles considered November to be one of the best months of the year. He knew some cooler weather was coming, and he always took the boys to a professional football game in November. But most important, he particularly enjoyed the feelings of Thanksgiving. He liked the way families came together to give thanks for the many blessings of the year.

Miles looked back on his year and realized he had much for which to be thankful. Sure, he had struggled with the news concerning his father's cancer, and he had dealt with the daily challenges of work and family. But overall, Miles had a thankful heart.

Although he was looking forward to celebrating Thanksgiving with his family and friends outside of work, he was particularly excited about sharing a meal with his team at work. Seth had made a deal with his team. He would make the turkey if they provided all the side dishes. Gabriela made the best sweet potato casserole, so he knew what his contribution would be.

OPPORTUNITY KNOCKS

Miles had finished his morning coffee and was headed to his computer station to start his shift when he saw Seth walk out of Hannah's office. Seth waved him over, so Miles headed straight to Hannah's office. Seth followed him into the office.

"What I'm about to tell you is not public knowledge, Miles," Hannah started as the two men sat down across from her desk. "We're about to have a management change. Jill has decided to leave her position as a manager and go back to being a call center rep."

"Wow," Miles replied looking first at Hannah and then at Seth, trying to look surprised. "I like Jill, and I've always heard she was a good manager. That's too bad it didn't work out for her."

"It's not that it didn't work out for her as far as we're concerned," Hannah replied. "This was Jill's choice. She simply wants to return to doing what she does best."

"As long as she's happy," Miles responded. After a moment of silence, he asked, "If this isn't public knowledge, why are you telling me?"

"We're conducting a search for her replacement," Hannah answered. "It should come as no surprise to you that we think a lot of you. You came to us with a lot of great experience, and you've shown leadership as a call center rep. Amanda Suttle saw a lot of potential in you, and she's got a pretty good track record of picking good talent. We think you would make a great manager, and we'd like to talk to you about replacing Jill."

Miles sat quietly for a moment. "I'm not sure what to say. I've been given the opportunity to accept a promotion before, but it was never the right time."

"How's the timing now?" Seth asked.

"I'm not sure," Miles answered. "My sons were always too young before. But now they're 13, which means they're heading into a lot more activities."

"There's no hurry," Hannah interjected. "Take some time and think about it. I'm sure you would want to talk it over with your wife. Just let us know when you're ready to talk about it some more."

Miles had told Mattie her news didn't affect him. Turns out he was wrong.

THE FUTURE

After his conversation with Hannah and Seth, Miles called Gabriela and asked her to get someone to watch the boys that evening so they could go out to dinner. He picked her up at the house, and they went to Reggiano's, one of the nicer restaurants in town.

"Nice," she said as she got out of the car. "You've either done something really wrong or you got a big promotion at work."

"Does it matter which one?" Miles joked as he closed his door.

"I'll tell you after you've paid for dinner," Gabriela smiled as they walked into the restaurant.

After they got settled, Miles shared his news. "I was offered a management job today."

"Where?" Gabriela asked. "It's been less than a year, and I really don't want to go through the hassles of moving again. And besides, the boys just turned 13 and it wouldn't be fair to . . ."

Miles held up his hand to stop her. "It would be in this office. We wouldn't have to move anywhere."

"Oh," Gabriela responded with a sigh of relief. "Then take it! A promotion means more money, right?"

"Not always," Miles responded. "But in this case, it would probably mean more money. But it would also mean a lot more work. Today I have specific shifts, and I can leave at the end of my shift. A promotion would mean an end to hourly work."

"That shouldn't be that big a deal," Gabriela responded.

"You say that now," Miles responded. "But when I miss the boys games or practices, or I can't be home at a specific time because you need me to do something, your opinion may change."

"Miles, uncertainty is a part of life. We always adjust, and we'll adjust to this as well."

"I know," Miles responded. "I just want to make the right decision for our family."

"Are you taking someone's place?"

"Yeah," Miles answered. "Jill Ramos."

"What happened?"

"Apparently she wanted to go back to being a call center rep. I heard she was promoted because she was the best call center rep at the time, not because she wanted to be a manager. Maybe she just wasn't cut out to be a manager."

"Do you think you're ready?"

"I'm not sure anyone knows whether they're ready until they get on the job," Miles responded. "Maybe I would feel more comfortable if I had been planning for it all along. I just always assumed I wouldn't be promoted."

"Why did you make that assumption?"

"Most people who get into management at Halifax have graduated from college. When I dropped out of college after a couple years, I just assumed I wouldn't get the opportunity to be in management."

"Well, get ready. This just may be your chance."

Miles was enjoying the dinner and conversation, but he knew he needed to get home so he could get some rest. He'd been tired lately with all the holiday activities. As much as he knew he needed to get rest, he found it wasn't always easy.

A PLEASANT FLASHBACK

Miles had spent most of the past week thinking about his conversation with Hannah and Seth. He was a planner, so he had made out his list of pros and cons. The most attractive aspect was the opportunity for a new challenge. The most unattractive aspect was a change in the relationship with his friends. Some people would say relationships don't have to change when someone gets promoted, but he knew they would.

There would be a time Miles would need to make a decision about his future with Halifax, but this day was about being thankful for what he had. His entire team had gathered in the conference room for a Thanksgiving feast. As he promised, Seth had provided a giant turkey, and his fellow team members all brought side dishes. By the time Miles finally got through the line, Gabriela's sweet potato casserole was gone. Her dish was a hit.

Miles had a flashback as he stood to the side watching everyone eat and laugh. It had been in this conference room in January where Seth had introduced himself to the team, where a handful of employees had sat at the conference table while most preferred to stand along the wall. Now, his fellow team members were fighting for a place to sit down. He saw that many of the changes had been implemented as a result of the Engagement Team proactively finding solutions to the challenges in the office, and he knew the management team had been working hard to create an environment where everyone wanted to be. Miles was confident the culture was the result of both management and the call center reps doing their part.

He looked over at Seth and knew he must be proud, knowing he helped create the culture that could make a difference in less than a year. A part of Miles wondered if he could do the same. It's one thing to stand on the sidelines of life and criticize managers for not doing enough to create a great environment. It's something else to get in the game and help make it happen.

DECISION TIME

Before Miles could sit down, he got a note from a shift coordinator instructing him to report to Hannah's office. When he walked in, Seth was already seated on the couch.

"Take a seat," Hannah motioned as she walked behind her desk. "We hadn't heard from you regarding our conversation last month, so we wanted to follow up with you. I know I told you to take your time, but we need to take some action on filling Jill's position. She's set to start her new job—or old job—on the first of January. Have you taken some time to think about it?"

"I have. In fact, my wife and I have talked about it on several occasions."

"And what have you concluded?" Seth asked from the couch.

"I've concluded that if a formal opportunity came along I would take it. I consider myself to be very engaged now, and believe I can become even more engaged if I took on a new opportunity to grow."

"Then consider this a formal opportunity," Hannah replied with a smile. "The promotion is yours if you want it."

"I'm honored," Miles smiled. "I look forward to working with both of you to learn how to keep the momentum going in this office."

"Okay, here's the deal. This news must remain private until we make a formal announcement next week. You can tell your wife, but that's it."

Miles sat quietly for a moment before he said, "I need a favor."

FAVOR GRANTED

The Dinner Club had started out with four people. For a brief period, the group had consisted of five, with the addition of Miles, and then went back to four when Larry decided to leave the group. No one else had ever joined the group, even as a visitor. It had become a place where a small group of co-workers could sit and talk about anything, with the knowledge that nothing ever left the table.

It was for that reason that Mattie was surprised to see Gabriela sitting at the table with Miles, Sydney, and Deanna when she arrived. "What a pleasant surprise to have you join us, Gabriela. You are so much better company than your husband!"

"I'm not staying for dinner," Gabriela replied. "I'm just here for a margarita, and . . ."

Miles interrupted her before she could finish. ". . . and a little announcement."

At that moment Hannah arrived at the table. She grabbed a chair from a nearby table and sat down next to Miles.

"And the surprises keep coming," Sydney laughed. "To what do we owe the pleasure?"

"I'm just here for a margarita . . ."

". . . and a little announcement," Mattie interrupted. "According to Miles, an announcement is being made. Do you happen to be a part of this little announcement?"

Just as Hannah was beginning to speak, the waiter arrived with a trayful of margaritas and passed them around the table. "Miles apparently planned ahead and ordered everyone a margarita to celebrate the news, and here it is: On Monday morning, we'll be announcing a change in management. One of the four managers is leaving—and no, it's not Seth—and your fellow team member and friend Miles Freeman is being promoted to management."

Everyone sat quietly for a second allowing the news to sink in. Sydney was the first to speak. "How long have you known about this, Miles?"

"Just found out yesterday. Hannah told me I could tell Gabriela, but that everyone else would have to wait. I asked her to come here to tell all of you. I was sworn to secrecy, and now you're being sworn to secrecy until Monday. You have become part of my family, and I wanted you to know before everyone else."

Sydney raised his glass toward the center of the table and waited for everyone else to join him. "Here's to my friend, Miles Freeman. May he enjoy all the success he deserves as a new manager."

"Hear! Hear!" They all joined in.

"I have one other favor to ask," Miles said as he looked toward Hannah and Gabriela. "Would you two please join us for dinner? When we're finished, we plan to look back on all the lessons we've learned this year, and we'd love to have you join us."

Both agreed. They all enjoyed a great dinner and even better conversation, and then the real Dinner Club began.

LESSONS LEARNED

"We've been through a lot this year," Miles started. "I came to this office and didn't know anyone. Deanna was the first person I met, sitting in the break room reading her Tom Clancy novel. Sydney was next, with an invitation to join this group. And because of him, I got to meet Mattie Brown."

Miles was silent for a moment before Mattie asked, "You're not going to mention Larry?"

"I am going to mention Larry," Miles smiled. "I was just trying to think of the most appropriate thing to say about him. He's hard to be around, but I learned something from him, and it ties directly into our training program. The relationships we develop in this world are so important, and it's imperative that we surround ourselves with the right people. This group came together so much more when we filtered out the negativity Larry brought to our group. We tried hard to find out what was troubling him, and he would never open up. I wish we had been successful in helping him, but we weren't. When we knew we couldn't succeed, we filtered out the negativity, and we're a better group today because of it. That's what I have to say about Larry, and that's the first lesson I learned this year."

"It sounds like you have another one to share," Sydney commented.

"I do, and maybe it's even more significant than the first. When I first came to this call center, I noticed a lot of call center reps were waiting for someone to make them happy. After going through the training and spending time looking at life satisfaction, I realize management really does have a limited role. They can recognize good performance and motivate us to continue, but they can't balance our lives or make us happy."

Sydney went next. "Great points, Miles. This has been a tough year for me. I've struggled with getting past my divorce while trying to raise my son by myself. I remember how last year I would sit around and complain about how bad things were for me, never taking personal responsibility for where I was in my life. This year has been different. The challenges aren't different, but the way I view them is. I used to blame work for my dissatisfaction, when, in reality, the way I was living the rest of my life never gave work a chance to succeed."

"What's changed for you?" Gabriela asked.

"The training we went through made me realize I was doing a pathetic job weaving everything together," Sydney answered. "I wasn't enhancing work relationships because I seldom did what I said I was going to do. I wasn't eating right or doing anything to take care of myself, so my physical health was lousy. I've been dragging around these anchors concerning my ex-wife, so my emotional health has been in shambles. I could go on and on, and could probably find something about every single aspect of my life that I ignored while I was blaming my job. And don't get me wrong—I still have a lot of work to do in every one of those areas. But at least I know what they are, and I can continue to head in the right direction."

"Wow," Hannah replied. "I had no idea the training had that kind of impact. I thought it was a simple life balance program. It sounds like it's had quite an impact on your life."

"It has had a huge impact, and so has this group. I'm just hoping my friend Miles doesn't get so wrapped up in his new management job that he forgets about all the efforts we're making."

"Just the opposite," Miles smiled. "I'm hoping to show others in the office the progress we've made and encourage others who may not have embraced the program to give it a try."

"Well, I guess I'll go next," Mattie said. "I learned a bunch, but two things in particular.

One, if I'm going to keep my emotional health under control, I have to learn to keep it all in perspective. As most of you know, my husband lost his job a few months ago. I thought our world was coming to an end. I realized that if I'm just willing to look around, I'll find a whole lot of people who have bigger struggles than that."

"Particularly at this time of year," Sydney responded.

"Exactly. And the second lesson is the one I shared with you at this table in October. A big part of my spiritual development has been committing to a cause greater than myself. Several things happened when my husband and I committed to helping the Alzheimer's organization. One, we gave ourselves a bigger purpose for our lives than work. Two, we've committed to financially support the organization, so when I wake up and don't want to go to work, I ask myself how I can support our organization if I'm not making the money to do it, and that gives me the motivation to get out of bed and go to work. Three, we've found a purpose for after we retire. We always wondered what we would do in retirement, and this provides the purpose. And four, others around us have seen what we're doing, and it's inspired them to do something similar."

"Gabriela and I are two of those people," Miles responded as he smiled at his wife. "We've been working with the American Cancer Society in our free time, and we're teaching the twins the importance of giving back at an early age."

"So, that's my story," Mattie said. "Still lots of work to do, but it's made a difference."

"Deanna," Miles smiled, "you've been very quiet tonight. What do you have to share?"

Deanna sat for a moment staring at the table before she began to share. "Mine is related to the first aspect of the training, the part about career. I left college after two years to figure out what I wanted to do for a living. For all of you, this is your career. For me, it's been a job as I've searched for what I want to do. I love it here, and I love the people I work with, but this isn't where my career should be spent."

"I'm not sure I like where this is heading," Mattie said.

"We learned that we have to ask the hard questions about our careers, like whether or not we're giving it our all. Perhaps one of the more difficult questions to ask is whether or not it's time for a change. I'm convinced that sometimes we do need to make a change. Dennis mentioned the need to have a connection between what we do, who we are, and what we value most in this life. I love working with kids, particularly those who have been dealt a lousy hand and are disadvantaged. I started volunteering at a home for abandoned and abused kids, and they've offered me a full-time job working in the office. So, I'm going to do what most people only dream about. I'm going to combine my passion and a way to make a living."

"Way too many changes tonight," Mattie said as she shook her head. "Miles gets promoted, and now Deanna is leaving. Sydney, our Dinner Club is falling apart. Are there any other announcements that need to be made tonight?"

Hannah began to smile. "Just one more, but I think you'll like this one. Seth asked me to tell you that your group won the challenge from the training in May. You had the best ideas, and you all get a day off from work. Sounds like you better hurry up and schedule it before you all go separate ways."

Separate ways. That wasn't something any of them wanted to think about.

GETTING SETTLED

Most weekends were exciting for Miles Freeman, but this past one was even better. His best friends from Dallas came in to celebrate New Year's Eve, so he got to ring in the New Year with good friends. Although he was enjoying time with his friends, he couldn't stop thinking about the new opportunity with his career.

Hannah had made the announcement about his promotion in December, but he wasn't set to start until the first Monday in January. He took the last week of the year off to spend with Gabriela and the twins, not certain what the New Year would have in store for him as he settled into his new job.

Miles arrived early on that Monday morning so he could get moved into Jill's office. The 8:00 AM managers' meeting had been rescheduled for 9:00 AM, so Miles had some extra time to get settled. He used some of the time to review the material Hannah had left on his desk related to *Engaged Leadership*, as well as the sheet of ideas created from the team suggestions. Before he headed out for his meeting, he posted it on the wall near the entrance to his cubicle.

FIRST MANAGERS' MEETING

Miles walked into the conference room right before 9:00 AM and sat down next to Seth. "Can I buy you lunch today? Since you just started as a manager a year ago, I was hoping you could give me some advice."

Before Seth could answer, Hannah walked in and started the meeting. Since Miles had been an interim manager before, he had a good idea what these managers' meetings were all about. They spent about an hour talking about reports and projects for the year. The training calendar was passed around for everyone to review. The entire office did another Employee Engagement Survey in December to see whether there was any improvement, and the report was due back in January.

After the meeting, Miles spent the rest of the morning scheduling one-on-one meetings with each member of his new team.

THE STUDENT BECOMES THE TEACHER

"I remember the first time I came over here," Miles remarked as he and Seth sat down at a table in the restaurant across the street from the office. "I came with Sydney and Mattie, and Sydney told me I'd be coming over here quite a bit. I think this is only the third time I've been here."

"The food's not that great," Seth smiled, "but it's convenient."

"So, you have a year of management experience," Miles started, "and you've had the chance to work for a leader who truly wanted to create a place where employees *want* to come. Are you glad they sent you here?"

"I'm not sure I could have had a better experience. I learned that management has a responsibility to create an environment where people want to be and that it doesn't have to be about beating them up to get them to work. And I also realized employees have a responsibility to bring something to the table to make employee engagement work."

"I plan to spend a lot of time over the next year picking your brain to figure out how to do this manager thing," Miles smiled. "I hope I don't wear you out with the questions."

They spent the rest of their lunchtime getting to know each other as peers now. Miles looked forward to learning from Seth's experiences. Sometimes plans just don't happen.

ONE MORE ANNOUNCEMENT

Miles walked back into his office, where he received his first sticky note from Hannah: "All managers in the conference room at 2:00 PM. —H."

Miles was in his seat talking with Aaron and Carmen when Hannah and Seth walked into the conference room together right at 2:00 PM. Hannah made the announcement that made Miles realize he wouldn't be leaning on Seth for guidance. Seth had been given a new assignment in a different city. Miles looked over and saw Carmen grinning from ear to ear as Hannah announced that Seth would finish out the month and report to his new job the first of February.

The time Miles had to learn from Seth just became significantly shorter.

A NEW DAY

Miles had expected his first month as a manager to be a learning experience. He just hadn't known how much he would need to cram into a one-month period. He was like a sponge as he soaked up as much information as possible in one-on-one meetings with Seth every day that month.

Miles learned a lot in those one-on-one meetings, but he also learned a lot just watching. He watched with pride as his friend Mattie was presented with a plaque for perfect attendance. And although he enjoyed being a part of sharing the good news about the drastic improvements the office had made with the Employee Engagement Survey, he felt a lot of disappointment when he saw Seth give Larry Marcus an opportunity to pursue a new career outside Halifax after he was let go. So many people had embraced the new culture, and Larry never had.

As Miles considered his new role as a manager, he knew one of his top priorities would be convincing his team of the importance—and simplicity—of life satisfaction. He knew it didn't need to be complicated.

As he headed out the door to greet his new team for the first time as a manager, he reached over and picked up a paperweight Seth had given him as a gift when his promotion was announced. It read:

Any intelligent fool can make things bigger and more complex. It takes a touch of genius—and a lot of courage—to move in the opposite direction.
—*Albert Einstein*

The Application of *Living for the Weekday*

I have someone I'd like you to meet. His name is Jeremy. He loves the weekend. He loves the freedom he feels Friday evening when he remembers he doesn't have to work the next day. He loves the satisfaction that comes from having an entire day with nothing on the agenda. He loves the thrill of knowing the plans he's made all week for a specific activity are finally about to happen. Oh yeah . . . Jeremy loves the weekend.

Then comes Sunday night and the realization that the joy of the weekend is coming to an end. That two-day respite Jeremy spent five days anticipating is now a memory, and he turns his attention to Monday's return to work.

He glares at the alarm clock Monday morning, then drags himself out of bed and wanders off to work to start the countdown to another weekend. He passes a coworker on the way into the office and growls, "Is it Friday yet?" On Tuesday, he moans to another coworker, "I can't wait until Friday." On Wednesday, he says with a grin, "It's Hump Day. We're halfway to Friday." On Thursday, his grin grows into a smile, and he says, "One more day to Friday!" And on Friday, with energy and enthusiasm, he beams, "It's Friday!!" And once again, the much-anticipated weekend is upon him.

You probably know somebody like Jeremy, or maybe you *think* like Jeremy. He is that employee who wastes five days of a seven-day week waiting for the weekend. Quite often, he looks forward to the weekend not because of any exciting plans he's made, but because he doesn't have to go to work.

Sadly, the excitement and delight with which Jeremy looks toward the weekend can be matched only by the angst and disdain he feels for returning to the weekday. It's as though he lives two different lives: one for himself and one for his job. And, if he's keeping score each week by days, he's losing.

On most Monday mornings, Jeremy drags himself to work to begin another five-day countdown to the weekend. Quite often, that dissatisfaction with his job translates to employee disengagement. In the fable, we learned that 74 percent of employees are at some level of disengagement, according to a study conducted by the Gallup Organization. Most are just disengaged, but nearly one in five is *actively* disengaged. As you can see, Jeremy is not alone.

Not many of us have a choice when it comes to work. If we prefer to live in a climate-controlled environment and have food readily available, *not* working is not an option. However, choosing to view our professional life in a new way *is* an option. Not only is it an option, it will be a requirement if we ever hope to overcome this epidemic of employee disengagement.

Jeremy is a real person—although his name has been changed—and in many ways he represents countless people I've met throughout my career. When I was initially putting together my thoughts for this book, I contacted him to share the premise for *Living for the Weekday.* When I told him what the book was about, he said, "Clint, I read your first book, and I liked what you wrote about leaders needing to create a culture to overcome employee disengagement. It sounds like now you're blaming the employees for the disengaged culture."

I explained to Jeremy there is a shared responsibility for overcoming employee disengagement. Yes, leaders must create a culture where employees want to be. They must build a consensus for the vision of the organization. They must inspire employees to want to pursue the vision. They must build a team to make it all happen. And they must do it with a character that no one can ever question. But at the same time, employees have a responsibility as well. There must be an effort for both sides to meet in the middle.

In my conversation with Jeremy that day, I shared with him the need for us to change the way we view our professional and personal lives coming together. As Miles and the team of employees at Halifax learned in the fable, anyone in search of a life that allows you to live for the weekday has a responsibility to focus on five areas of life. The five areas of *Living for the Weekday* are *Career*, *Relationships*, *Health*, *Finances*, and *Spirituality*.

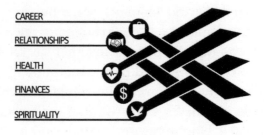

It is based on a woven fabric. The idea behind the image is that life satisfaction is more about weaving the most important things in your life together than it is about balance. You'll never have perfect balance between the five aspects of your life, because you have different priorities at different points in your life.

Real balance is, by definition, an equality of distribution. When you examine the five aspects, an equal distribution will never be achieved—nor would it be responsible to encourage it. To even chase this imaginary concept of life balance is irritating at best. Instead, we should be aware of how these five facets of our lives are woven and stitched together, and how each has an affect on the others.

By keeping an eye on these fives aspects, we can normally find the root of any challenge. Sometimes we think we've accurately identified the aspect of our life that is causing discomfort because we see the challenge right under our nose. Quite often, it's not the challenge that's the problem. It's what is lacking in life that's the problem.

Finally, the concepts in this book are not difficult. They don't need to be. Many people want some novel approach for gaining balance in their lives. They want some radical new idea to try. The truth is simple—we haven't gotten good at the old things.

Keep in mind that our success in this world will not be determined by what we know. Our success in this world will be determined by what we do. As with everything in life, the key to capitalizing on *Living for the Weekday* will be in the application of the ideas, not in their complexity.

In the fable, Miles helps his coworkers understand the five aspects of life. To support you in your effort to put these ideas to work in your life, I offer these lessons as challenges within the five areas of *Living for the Weekday*. In addition, I offer some specific action items along with each challenge.

Here we go. Let's start with *Career*.

CAREER

So much of our lives are consumed by our careers. Your career should be an enjoyable experience that makes use of your expertise and talents in a valuable way. It should not only be a good utilization of your skills and abilities, it should be a place you enjoy going to be around people you enjoy being around. It *should* be all those things, but quite often it's not.

My hope is that every one of you may find a career that brings you immense joy. After all, it is an integral part of life. It helps define who we are, and it is a primary source of social standing. Despite my hope that each person reading these pages may find a career that brings him or her immeasurable joy, it won't happen. In fact, it won't happen for many people.

Most of our waking hours are spent at work, yet according to the Bureau of Labor Statistics, 67 percent of American workers are unhappy in their present work situation. The reasons for dissatisfaction are all over the board. Some people dislike their boss, while others dislike their colleagues. Some people dislike the actual work they perform, while others aren't experiencing enough of a challenge. Perhaps they're just angry the job didn't turn out the way it *should* be.

I'm curious about the 67 percent who don't like their work environment but keep showing up year after year. I'm also curious about the 33 percent who somehow find a way to be happy. While conducting research for this book, I held a few informal interviews with some people I consider to be on both ends of the spectrum. I selected the comments of two individuals who seemed to be representative of their group. Again, one falls within the 67 percent, and one falls within the 33 percent.

Let's start with the person I interviewed who loved her job. We'll call her Karen, which is convenient, because that's her name. She's part of the 33 percent. I wanted to know whether she had lower standards than all the others. After all, who actually *likes* their job? I wanted to know whether she had a better relationship with the boss. I wanted to know whether she had learned how to play the game so everyone got along, or whether she was paid more than everyone else. Most important, I wanted to know whether there was something I could learn from her.

I spoke with Karen for just over an hour, then edited her remarks to summarize the recurring themes from our conversation:

First of all, I appreciate the fact I have a job. Unemployment is high right now. Every morning as I walk through those doors, I picture all the people who don't have a job and would gladly take my place. I get paid well to do my job, and it's a pretty easy commute. As for the actual work, it's not all that thrilling, but I knew I wasn't changing the world when I took the job.

There are two observations I'd like to make. One, she brought up some things I think contribute to job satisfaction for many people—she is paid well, has an easy commute, and knew what she was getting into when she took the job. And two, the most significant thing she mentioned was appreciation. Based on her comments, I realized job *satisfaction* starts with job *appreciation*. In fact, appreciation *for* the job was the first step toward being satisfied *with* the job. How many people do you know who will never be satisfied with the job because they will never be appreciative of the job?

Now let's look at the person I interviewed who didn't like his work environment. His name is Glenn. He's part of the 67 percent who don't like their work yet keep showing up year after year. I struggled to edit his remarks to a paragraph, unsure of how to get that much negativity into a single paragraph:

This place wears me out. I'm sick of all the politics, and I'm sick of all the changes. It's nothing like it used to be. I work 60-hour workweeks every month, and when I'm not working, I'm stressing about what I have to do when I go back to work. I've put in a lot of time, and this company owes me big.

There are many observations I could make, but I'm going to limit my observations to two. One, his feeling the company "owes me big" is part of a much bigger entitlement mentality that exists in many organizations. Employees who have served for many years—and some who have not been around all that long—have this feeling the company owes them something more than they've received. Let me be clear about this. Companies owe us the compensation they agreed to pay us when we do the work we agreed to do. Beyond that, we settle up every two weeks. And two, things change. In many ways, technology has made things worse, not better. Long-term loyalty is a thing of the past—for employees and employers. Some companies raise their expectations, expecting more and more, yet offering less and less. Things change. We must find a way to get past it, and walking around the hallways of your employer complaining to anyone who will listen is not the way to get past it. Becoming a part of the disengaged crowd is not the way to get past it. You must either find a way to enjoy the game or get out of the game.

Finally, as much as I want you to find a career that brings you joy, and as much as *you* want to find a career that brings you joy, there is a simple reality many people never realize: No one ever said you get to have a job you love. If you aren't in the job you love today, then get out there and search for it. But in the meantime, you have to *do* the job you're in.

There are many ways to enhance your career—or your job, if you haven't found a career at this point in your life—and I'd like to challenge you to do two things in this *Career* section.

CHALLENGE ONE: ADDRESS THE HARD QUESTIONS ABOUT YOUR CAREER

According to the Gallup poll referenced earlier, three out of four employees are at some level of disengagement. Too many people are working jobs they hate, dealing with people they can't stand. They drag themselves to work every day, often pointing the finger of blame at others for their own dissatisfaction. They are giving a fraction of their full potential every time they walk through the doors of their employer. There are many questions that need to be asked and answered—by employers and employees—to determine why so much dissatisfaction is taking place.

Employers need to address some hard questions. Are you paying people a fair wage? Are you providing competitive benefits? Do employees know what is expected of them? Are you providing the employees the tools to do their jobs? Are you recognizing employees for their efforts? Are you soliciting the opinions of your employees? Are you telling employees how they're doing? The list could go on and on.

Employees need to address some hard questions as well. Certainly they need to determine whether they're happy in the career—or job—they've chosen to accept. But there are some harder questions that need to be considered.

To get you started, here are some recommended questions to ask about your career:

❏ *Are you giving it your all?* At some point you accepted the opportunity to work in your current role. You agreed to perform a duty, and the company agreed to pay you for your work. Regardless of what you think about the amount of work you provide compared to the amount of compensation you receive, you made a deal when you took the job. So, at some point, you must conduct an honest assessment of your performance. Here goes: Are you giving it your all? Honestly, are you giving it your all? Are you doing your job to the best of your ability? Are you giving an honest day's work for an honest day's pay? Are you surpassing your boss's expectations? Are you surpassing your *own* expectations? I'm certain there have been times you've gone above and beyond what was expected. You produced outstanding work and delivered way more value than you were paid for. But I'm talking about day in and day out. When we don't feel we're giving it everything we have—even when we think we're justified—it's easy to become disengaged. If you're not giving it your all, could that be the reason you're disengaged?

❏ *Would a different job matter?* A lot of people are looking for other job opportunities. With two-thirds of employees unhappy in their current work environment and three out of four disengaged in their work, it's no huge surprise. As I indicated earlier, if you aren't in the job you love, then get out there and search for it. You aren't doing yourself any favors by being miserable; you aren't doing your employer and the people you work with any favors; and you certainly aren't doing the customers of the company you serve any favors. I'm curious what people are hoping to find. Greener grass, maybe? As we all know, the grass is not always greener on the other side, and when it is, it's usually because it's received a lot of attention and required a lot more work. Could making a job change make any difference at all, or would you carry the same disengagement to another job? Yes, there are things a boss can do to create a culture of engagement, but if you don't show up at the new job in the right frame of mind, the only thing that will change about your new job will be the commute.

❏ *Is it time for a change?* Many people blame their job for the dissatisfaction in their life, and sometimes that is indeed the case. Although there's a good chance that dissatisfaction in your life is coming from someplace other than work, the reality is that some people are simply in the wrong job. Maybe they lack the skill to make a significant contribution. Maybe they lack the knowledge of the industry to get the bigger picture. Maybe they lack the resources to get the job done. Or maybe they just lack the motivation to deal with a lousy boss or the politics that always seem to get in the way. Perhaps they started a "job" and stayed there so long it became what they thought was a "career." Whatever the reason, anyone in a miserable job should ask whether it's time for a change. If you can work through your challenges at your current employer, work them out. It may be true that no one promised you a job you would love, but you have the opportunity to go find one you love.

These are just a few of the hard questions that need to be addressed. Once you determine the answers to these questions, you likely will uncover a whole new set of questions. And as long as you're asking the hard questions that point the finger of blame back at yourself for dissatisfaction in your career, then you're headed toward finding more career satisfaction.

CHALLENGE TWO: FOCUS ON YOUR OWN PERSONAL GROWTH

Years ago I was giving a late-afternoon speech in Las Vegas. I couldn't fly out until the next morning, so I attended an awards dinner with the employees of the company.

After the awards program concluded, I was leaving the ballroom and was stopped by a young lady in the hallway. She said, "I have a quick question for you, Clint." I recognized her from the afternoon session, so I was prepared to answer a question regarding the content of the program.

"What did you learn today?" she asked. Somewhat surprised and confused by her question, I responded, "What do you mean?"

She replied, "You gave a great presentation today. While your humor made us laugh, your content challenged us to really think about the way we approach our work. And since you mentioned the importance of learning in the program, I'm curious what *you* learned today."

This young lady was by far the youngest person in the audience that day, and she was astute enough to ask a very profound and fair question. I thought about it for a moment, answered her question, and returned to my room for the night.

Every day is a learning opportunity. We learn through unexpected, everyday occurrences. We learn because an organization makes an investment in our future. We learn because we choose to pursue our own opportunities for education.

There are some jobs that don't require any prior training. However, most job opportunities require some basic, foundational skills. In fact, you were probably required to bring certain skills to the table when you initially got the job you're in today. But here's my question for you. What have you done to enhance your skills? How much of your own time and money have you invested in your own development?

You should be taking steps every day to do things to further your own education. Why? Two reasons. One, it helps you add value as an employee, and bosses often appreciate and take care of employees who add value. And two, it prepares you for new and different opportunities that could bring you more job satisfaction. The bottom line is this: The quickest way to improve your situation is to improve yourself.

To get you started, here are some recommended action items to help you focus on your own personal growth:

☐ *Pursue training offered by your company.* Most large organizations offer training opportunities to employees at all levels, as do some smaller companies that understand the importance of human capital. If you have access to employer-provided training opportunities, take advantage of them. I am amazed at the number of people who don't take advantage of training opportunities. Sadly, I encounter clients all the time who tell me they are making training sessions mandatory, just to get people to attend. If it's offered, take it. Find opportunities to enhance your performance in the job you have today, and take classes that offer transferable skills as well.

☐ *Take advantage of online training opportunities.* There was a time when learning outside of a job required going back to school. If you can go back to school and pursue education in a specific field, do it. If time or cost is an issue, go online. There are so many educational opportunities right at your fingertips if you're just willing to search for them. Some will cost you money, but many are offered at no cost. Again, look for transferable skills. Perhaps one of the best things you can do is to learn a new language. Some people will say, "Why should I spend my time trying to learn something new? The company should be offering it." Why should you be spending your time trying to learn something new? Because it's *your* life and you have the responsibility to make the most of it. So, log off the 15 social media sites you visit each day long enough to learn something new.

☐ *Read a book a month.* The fact you're reading this book at this very moment indicates you have an interest in learning something—or perhaps that it was mandatory reading and someone is forcing you to educate yourself. Perhaps one of the best self-paced methods of learning is reading a book. No class time, no professors, and no exams. Books are readily available. Get them free from a library. Get them discounted online and at bookstores. Borrow them from a friend. They're all around, so you have no excuse. Make a commitment to read a book a month. Finish this one and you're finished for the month!

It's your life. It's your career. You can choose to sit around and wait for someone to make it great for you, or you can take some steps to improve it on your own. Ask the hard questions about your career, and focus on your own personal growth. Ultimately, you'll be taking responsibility for your own career satisfaction.

RELATIONSHIPS

Among the most significant aspects of our lives are the relationships we enjoy. Whether you openly seek strong relationships or stubbornly avoid them, we all require companionship at home and work. These relationships often impact our success or failure in many aspects of life.

While relationships are important and may have an impact, our success or failure in this world is our own. But the relationships we enjoy can enhance the experience. A strong relationship with someone at work can make a tedious or boring job more enjoyable. A strong relationship can provide the accountability to live a healthy lifestyle. A strong relationship at home is required to discuss the often private issue of finance, and a strong relationship can help deepen the spiritual side of our life. As you can see, relationships affect each of the other aspects of your life.

Despite the importance of strong relationships in our lives, the pace at which many people live life has made relationships a much lower priority. Many of us are so focused on the things we believe we can handle on our own that we ignore the very social support systems in relationships that can help us lead a more satisfying life.

You may recall from the fable the comment Larry Marcus made regarding the relationships in his life: "I have plenty of friends, and I don't need to make more friends at work. In fact, I intentionally don't make friends at work so I can just go in and get my job done. The quicker I can get it done, the sooner I can get off work and go home to my real friends."

His comment was sad on so many levels. One, this is a prime example of how employees separate home life and work life, then wonder why they despise going to work on a Monday morning. Two, we have a need to connect with others, and the lack of a connection with others at work will lead to disengagement and a countdown to the end of the day. And three, effective work relationships often determine promotions and pay increases because of the information shared in those relationships.

While the importance of relationships at work is obvious on many levels, relationships away from work—or the lack of relationships—often affect our job satisfaction without us even knowing it. You see, it's hard to be enthusiastic about work when we leave for work in the middle of a fight with a significant person in our life and realize the fight will continue the moment we get home. It's hard to be enthusiastic about work when we spend the day text messaging friends about various disagreements because we can't work out the issues.

There are many ways to enhance the relationships in your life—both at work and home—and I'd like to challenge you to do two things in this *Relationships* section.

CHALLENGE THREE: SURROUND YOURSELF WITH THE RIGHT PEOPLE

One of the most important decisions we make in life is who we choose to be around. In fact, there is an old proverb that reads, "Show me your friends and I'll tell you who you are." Quite often we become like the people we're around. Based on that, we must be cautious about whom we surround ourselves with because of the short- and long-term implications.

Years ago I worked with a lady who needed to hear this information. She hung around a group of actively disengaged employees. She would wait for her break so she could hang around the negative crowd and talk about how bad things were. Do you know people like her? She hung around people who didn't like their job, their boss, or the company, and she became like them. Do you know people like her? If you hang around people who don't like their jobs, you'll become like them. If you hang around people who don't care about growing in the company, you won't grow in the company.

To get you started, here are some recommended action items to help you surround yourself with the right people:

- ❐ *Analyze your crew.* We lean on our friends a lot. We share our successes and challenges with them. It's important these people be the ones who support and encourage us. We must find a support system of friends who will support and challenge us. In the fable, Miles and his fellow team members used the Dinner Club as a way of supporting each other. Do an analysis of your circle of friends and see whether they add to your life or take away from it. Surround yourself with people who will help you reach your goals. If you want to be financially successful, surround yourself with those who are financially successful. If you hang out with people who are broke, you'll never learn how people who aren't broke live their lives. If you want to improve your relationship with your spouse, surround yourself with people in successful relationships.

- ❐ *Filter out the negativity.* We live in a world that surrounds us with negativity. We get it regularly from media outlets because it sells. There is no shortage of it from the people around you every day. Coworkers, bosses, subordinates, friends, family, and strangers on the street will seek you

Handwritten margin notes:

① Support encourage challenge us

② Run away negative friends

③ Delicate time to interact with people who means most with us.

out to share the crud in their lives. While it is my
hope that we all will take the time to support
people in need when challenges are presented,
these are not the situations to which I am referring. I am referring to the people in our lives who
drain us of our energy because they thrive on
sharing their own negativity. Refuse it. Don't just
walk away from the negativity—run. Get as far
away from it as you can. Not only does it impact
our perspective with regard to our own lives, it
impacts our mental health. While your success
can be determined in part by whom you surround
yourself with, it can also be determined in part by
whom you choose to *not* surround yourself with.

☐ *Dedicate time to the relationships.* One of the
reasons we dread going back to work on Monday is we don't feel we've spent enough time
with the people who matter. Our lives are so
busy that sometimes we have to dedicate the
time to interact with the people who mean the
most to us. If you need to schedule time to keep
in touch with friends and family, put it on a
calendar. Some may say, "But Clint, my calendar is full." Sometimes we have to make hard
choices about what to eliminate in order to
dedicate time to the relationships.

If you're around someone with a cold, there's a
good chance you'll catch the cold. What are you
catching from the people around you? These relationships in your professional and personal life are
as important to your job satisfaction as the work

itself. Do everything in your power to surround yourself with the right people.

CHALLENGE FOUR: ENHANCE WORK RELATIONSHIPS

The choice to surround ourselves with the right people is a powerful choice. Just as people in our personal lives have a profound impact on our business lives, so do the people we work around. If you cannot get along with the people around you at work, you will never live for the weekday.

While we may be able to control those who surround us in our personal lives, that's not always the case in our professional lives. However, work relationships can be enhanced by the actions you take and the behaviors you exhibit at work.

To get you started, here are some recommended action items to help you enhance work relationships:

- ☐ *Do what you say you're going to do.* Sometimes we do work that is independent of our co-workers, but in larger organizations our work is often interrelated in some way. The work of the people around you is often affected when commitments are met—and not met. Keep your commitments, and do what you say you're going to do. Meet a deadline even if it requires extra effort. Show up at work even when you don't want to go. It's not all about you. Others are depending on you to keep your commitments.

On the rare occasion you can't, communicate the reason and fix it. You will enhance relationships when the people you work with know you are dependable.

☐ *Lift up the people around you.* We all want to be recognized for a job well done. Too often, we sit around waiting for a boss to create an inspired culture. As a part of the team, praise your co-workers when they do a great job. Compliment them for keeping commitments and meeting deadlines that help you do your job well. If you're lucky, they may just return the recognition some day. And if they don't, it's okay. Your motivation should be to enhance the relationship with your coworkers by lifting them up when they do well, not to solicit reciprocal praise for a job well done.

☐ *Don't point the finger.* Every organization has a person or two who is famous for pointing the finger of blame at others when things go wrong. Don't be that person. Your goal should be to provide solutions to problems, not alienate the people you work with—or for—by pointing the finger of blame.

The people we're around either add to our life satisfaction or they take away from it. They can hold us accountable and encourage us to live to a higher standard, or they can allow us to break the rules and eliminate any standards at all. Build relationships that make a positive difference in your life.

HEALTH

Few people would ever downplay the importance of health in their lives. In fact, an old proverb reads, "He who has health has hope, and he who has hope has everything." We all want to be healthy, and we normally desire the same for the people we know. In fact, a very common toast includes a wish for good health.

It is my hope that you enjoy good health in your life. In fact, I hope your good health allows you to find satisfaction in your day-to-day life so it can enhance your professional life. Sadly, for many people holding this book that probably will not happen.

Health is often the first thing we push to the side as we hurry through our fast-paced lives. Our hectic travel schedules have us eating on-the-go meals and zipping through fast-food drive-through restaurants. The fast-paced world in which we live has us moving so quickly that we sacrifice eating healthy for eating quickly. Ironically, some people work all day, and in an effort to "balance" their work life and home life, they race home with an unhealthy bag of food so they can sit down and have quality time with their families.

This lack of focus on our physical and emotional health often results in lack of productivity on the job. This lack of productivity inevitably leads to disengagement.

Health is critical to our overall satisfaction— both physical and emotional health. Not only is it required to live a long, vibrant life, it makes us feel better. And the better you feel, the better you look. And the better you look, the more energy you have.

There was a time in my life I had everything I wanted. I had the job I wanted and earned an income I thought was fair for my contributions to the organization. I lived in the house I wanted and drove the car I wanted. Everything seemed to be going my way. There was just one small problem. Every day when I woke up I felt lousy.

When I graduated from high school I was six feet tall and weighed 118 pounds. I had the highest metabolism of anyone on the globe. As a result, I didn't focus on my health. I could eat what I wanted and drink what I wanted, and it never had an impact on my weight. As I got older, I had to change my habits.

My wife and I have three dogs. Although we watch what we eat, we take better care of our dogs than we do of ourselves. Our dogs eat the best food made for dogs. I have three dogs, and I've never called them to dinner and put down a plate of pizza and a cold beer—although I'm sure they'd be happy to try it—and then filled the plate up two or three times before bedtime.

Our health—both physical and mental—helps determine our overall satisfaction with life, as well as our level of engagement on the job. This area deserves as much attention as any of the others.

There are many ways to enhance your health, but I'd like to challenge you to do two things in this *Health* section.

CHALLENGE FIVE: FOCUS ON YOUR PHYSICAL HEALTH

A focus on physical health is a first step toward emotional health. You see, the mind and body are linked. When the body is improved, an improvement in emotional well-being is seen as well.

To get you started, here are some recommended action items to help you focus on your physical health:

- ☐ *Get more rest.* Most people need seven to eight hours of sleep each night in order to be on top of their game. Somewhere along the way it became cool to brag about how little sleep we get. I used to know a guy who ran around bragging about how he needed only three to four hours of sleep a night. Don't listen to these people. Get more sleep. Sleep is our body's recovery time. Not getting enough sleep means you will not have the right kind of energy to work efficiently. And, as a side note, do not use this as an excuse to be lazy. Get the rest you need, then get up and get to work.

☐ *Learn about nutrition and practice it.* This is not a nutrition book, so it's not the place to determine what you should be doing with your daily diet. However, if you truly want to have your health contribute to a more satisfied life, then you need to learn as much as you can about nutrition. There are many people who can teach you. If you can afford it, hire a nutritionist. If you can't afford it, go online and find a free resource. Get your hands on a nutrition book. Turn on a cooking channel and learn how to cook some healthy food. Get in a habit of eating healthy meals—it's been said we should eat breakfast like a king, lunch like a prince, and dinner like a pauper. Find ways to do that. I'm not encouraging you to become a health nut. I want you to work toward a healthy lifestyle. I travel for a living, and airports aren't known for having numerous alternatives for healthy eating. You'll probably see me in a fast-food line, but as often as possible I'll be looking at the healthier choices on the menu. Two-thirds of Americans are overweight. Don't be a part of the statistic. Learn about nutrition and practice it.

☐ *Get off the couch.* You've heard it all your life— eat less, exercise more. Once you've learned about nutrition and started practicing it, focus on your physical activity. If you have the time and resources to join a gym, do it. Along with that, hire a trainer. However, don't allow money—or the lack of money—to be your excuse. If you can't afford a gym or a trainer, find other ways to add activity to your day. Walk during your lunch break. Take the stairs instead of the elevator. For me, as I travel through airports, I don't ride the moving walkways. Small, but it works for me. If you can dedicate 30 minutes a day, great. If not, find those small ways to make a difference. Exercise can do much more than help you watch your weight. It can improve your mood, reduce your stress, and boost your energy level. Exercise not only strengthens our heart and lungs, it also strengthens our emotional health. In a nutshell, the choices we make every day regarding our physical activities affect the way we feel physically *and* emotionally.

Our lives are more hectic now than ever before. In order to perform all the duties and meet all the demands of a hectic life, we must have a healthy and strong body. Ultimately, your health affects everything else in your life.

CHALLENGE SIX: FOCUS ON YOUR EMOTIONAL HEALTH

For the record, I am not a psychologist, and in no way am I qualified to address the deep issues related to mental health and the impacts it has on your job. The role a job or career plays in many people's lives can cause serious mental health issues, which can affect many aspects of those lives. Anyone who feels emotionally unstable should seek help from a professional in that field, not from the author of a business book.

However, I would like to address what I've experienced regarding emotional health and job satisfaction from working with people over the past two decades. It seems to me that people who are in control of their emotions and behaviors seem to find job satisfaction much easier than those who believe they have no control over their emotions. They tend to feel good about themselves and the people around them.

Some people seem to live very fortunate lives and never have a challenge. They seem to be emotionally strong because it just comes easily for them. But just as we have a responsibility to work out to maintain our physical health, we can do things to boost our emotional health.

To get you started, here are some recommended action items to help you focus on your emotional health:

☐ *Cut loose the anchors from your past.* We drag around so much crud from our past. Some people hang onto grudges as though they're increasing in value and will one day be worth a small fortune. The reality is, we waste so much energy dragging things around behind us. If you want to increase your life satisfaction, cut loose the anchors that are holding you back. Forgive someone who has hurt you. If you can't do it for them, do it for yourself. We are over-looked for a promotion, and we pout about it for years. We aren't recognized by a boss, and we think about it every time we see him. We don't get a bonus one year, and we think about it every time we open a check. Get over it. Cut loose the anchors in all aspects of your life, because you drag that stuff to work every day.

❑ *Keep it all in perspective.* No matter how bad you have it in your life, there is always someone who has bigger problems. Keep it all in perspective. According to research, more than 50 percent of the world's population lives on less than two dollars a day. Think about that the next time you start to complain about your finances.

❑ *Make yourself a priority.* People are working, raising children, building businesses, and trying to keep up with life. Everyone around us seems to be a priority. At some point, we must make ourselves a priority. Take time for yourself. Find a hobby that challenges you. Find a spot where you can go to get away from all the distractions of life. Schedule a massage. Take a nap. Whatever it is, make it about you, so you have the chance to reenergize and reload.

Legendary baseball player Mickey Mantle once said, "If I knew I was going to live this long, I would have taken better care of myself." I suppose we all feel that way at some point in our lives. Achieving a level of satisfaction in life requires good health, and those around you hoping you find that satisfaction are depending on you to take steps in that direction.

FINANCES

Oh, the pursuit of the almighty dollar. I'm sure the percentage of people who jump out of bed and head to work for any reason other than earning an income is very small. In fact, it would be a safe bet that most people would quit their jobs if they no longer had a need for money. I'm not aware of many lottery winners who continue in a job they don't love.

As long as we have bills to pay, we need to find a way to earn an income. It is my hope you make all the money you can count. It is my hope you enjoy so much success you become financially independent. These are my hopes for you because that's what you want, right? Like most people, you pursue the almighty dollar because once you've obtained enough money you will finally be happy, right?

Research conducted at the University of Chicago's National Opinion Research Center contradicts that assumption. According to the research, disposable income for the average American has grown about 80 percent since 1972, but the percentage of respondents describing themselves as "very happy" (approximately one-third) has hardly budged over the years. We have convinced ourselves that more money will make us happy, but those who actually achieve that seldom claim that money alone made them happy.

Sadly, most people won't ever know whether a lot of money would make them happy because most people do a lousy job of managing their finances. Rather than taking the personal responsibility required to enhance the management of their finances, they complain they don't make enough. Rather than adjusting their lifestyle to fit the income they generate, they complain the company doesn't pay them what they're worth.

Here's a fact. There will be days when your contribution to the company is much greater than the compensation you receive for your efforts. There will be days when you will work so many hours and make so many sacrifices that you'll feel underpaid. And in some cases, you just may be right. But be honest about how you answer this next question. Are there ever days you do less than an honest day's work for an honest day's pay? Are there times when you give about half the effort you know you could? And on those occasions, have you ever gone to the HR manager and asked that person to adjust your pay *downward* for those periods? All we can do is hope that it all evens out in the long run.

This isn't a financial planning book, and I'm not a financial planner, so I promise I won't go into detail about how you need to manage your money. However, I am a leadership development consultant who understands the influence money has on our lives and the significant impact it has on everything we're trying to weave together to find more happiness.

There are many ways to enhance the financial aspect of your life, but I'd like to challenge you to do two things in this section on *Finance*.

CHALLENGE SEVEN: TIE FINANCES TO YOUR BIGGER GOALS

I remember my first year out of college. I went to work for a great company that paid me a fair salary. I wasn't married and didn't have children, so I didn't have family expenses. I lived in an apartment, so I didn't have the maintenance expenses that went with home ownership. Needless to say, I had disposable income.

It was a great year. I worked hard, and I enjoyed my life. At the end of that year, I had absolutely nothing to show for it. Like many people, I looked around and wondered where all my money had gone. I didn't think I had been frivolous with my money, but I still didn't have anything of value after earning a decent salary for a full year.

It didn't take me long to realize I needed to have something to show for my efforts. I certainly wasn't getting rich in corporate America, but I was doing well enough to pay my bills and plan for my future. I knew what I wanted to do with my life and had identified my bigger goals. I needed to tie my financials to those bigger goals.

To get you started, here are some recommended action items to help you tie financials to your bigger goals:

❒ *Learn how to manage your money.* Some people make a truckload of money every two weeks, and some make enough to get by. Regardless of your income level, you must learn to manage your money. We like to complain that we don't make enough money, but I wonder sometimes if it's just that we don't know how to handle what we have. Our inability to manage our finances leads to a lack of financial security, which is ultimately what makes us uncomfortable. As I indicated earlier, I am not a financial planner, so I'm not going to offer up financial advice. There are many people out there who can do that for you. And if you can't afford them, go online and find a free resource. Buy a book. If you can't afford that, borrow a book. Take a Dave Ramsey course. Have someone teach you how to create and stay within a budget. Have someone teach you how to get out of debt, save money, and plan for your retirement. When we do a better job of managing our money, we find ways to be happy with the money we make. When we do a better job of managing our money, we enhance relationships and reduce stress. Ultimately, it gives us a sense of security and peace of mind.

❒ *Stop comparing yourself to those around you.* No matter how much money you make, there will always be someone you know who makes more than you. No matter what you buy, there will always be someone you know who buys something better than you. At some point in my life, I realized two things. One, people with money fall into two categories: rich and wealthy. People who are rich *make* a lot of money. People who are wealthy *have* a lot of money. Given the choice, I'd prefer to *have* a lot of money. Two, the people who buy a lot of stuff are usually the rich people, many of whom are one missed paycheck away from the moving van pulling into their driveway and taking it all away, and I don't want to be like those people. Some people get into that position because they're greedy, but most get there because they compare themselves to those around them. Stop comparing yourself financially to people around you and live your life based on what's important to you.

☐ *Pick a target and start your plan.* There is something you would like to have in your life. It may be a material item, or it may be a place you'd like to visit. Maybe it's your dream car or an expensive piece of jewelry. Maybe it's an international trip you've wanted to take or a gift you've wanted to buy for a loved one. Or maybe it's to save a cash reserve or get out of debt forever. Whatever it is, it will require a financial commitment. Identify it right now, and start your plan to save for it. It needs to be in line with managing your money, and it needs to be a goal you can work toward every time you get a paycheck. Throughout my career, I've had a few jobs—and bosses—I didn't particularly like. It was during these times that I used my target—and the need for financial support to reach it—as the motivation to get out of bed and go to work.

You owe it to yourself, your family, and your employer to get this part right. It simply is not possible to be worried about your finances and focused on your job at the same time. We must tie our financials to our bigger goals.

CHALLENGE EIGHT: ADD MORE VALUE TO YOUR EMPLOYER

There should be only one reason an employer keeps you around . . . you add value to the organization. Jobs are lost every day for a myriad of reasons, but the most common is that the person being handed the pink slip is simply not seen as valuable to the organization. Simply put, when your salary is more than the value you provide, you need to start worrying.

The first priority should always be to keep your job. If you are successful at keeping your job, the best chance of improving your financial situation comes from adding more value to your employer. Here's the great news. Most employees simply show up at work, do the bare minimum to get by, collect a paycheck, and go home. The competition isn't that great in most organizations to go above and beyond to add additional value to your employer.

To get you started, here are some recommended action items to help you add more value to your employer:

- *Find new ways to make or save money for your employer.* Organizations strive to make a profit in two ways: (1) Create income and/or (2) save expenses. For that matter, even nonprofit organizations operate with these goals in mind. When you can show an employer how to do either one of these two things, you add more value as an employee, and it makes you more attractive to your employer.
- *Become a solution-finder.* Some employees have been led to believe it is their job to find problems. While some jobs may be designed for employees to find problems, most are designed for employees to identify solutions. Unless you've been hired for one of those unique jobs where you sit around all day and look for problems, show up every day with the intention to find solutions. If there are other humans at your job, then politics are at play and things don't always go as planned. However, keep in mind that, in most cases, solution finders are recognized. Solution finders are promoted. Solution finders receive raises. Solutions earn the respect and admiration of the people you work with.
- *Make your case, and then ask for a raise.* Many people walk in and ask for a raise. Those who receive the raises are typically the ones who

have proven they add value to the organization. The people who receive the raises are not always the ones who have worked the hardest or longest. Cost-of-living adjustments generally go to those employees who have met expectations. Raises generally go to those who have gone above and beyond the expectations of their employer by adding additional value to the organization.

According to a study by salary.com, 65 percent of employed survey respondents said they are looking around at other job opportunities. The survey doesn't break down the reasons, but I'm certain some of those respondents are looking for more money. Money is a focus whether we like it or not.

SPIRITUALITY

As was mentioned in the fable, *spirituality* is a word with many meanings. Your definition will be determined in part by how you were raised and at which stage of life you are in at this point. For some people, it's as formal as organized religion. To others, it's less structured and more open to new influences in the world.

It is not my intent to change what you think about spirituality or how you define it. After all, this book is designed to help you enjoy your work and life more and to encourage you to live for the weekday. There are many definitions of *spirituality*, so rather than trying to narrowly define a word that has many meanings, I want to address the importance of our spirituality—regardless of what that may mean for you—and how it connects to our work.

Some people do everything they can to separate their spiritual and their work lives, and I'm convinced that's not possible. You see, there must be a connection between what we do, who we are, and what we value most in this life. For most people, what they *do* is their job, and who they *are* comes from their spirituality. Therefore, there must be a connection between your career and your faith.

Some people argue there are so many different aspects and definitions of spirituality that the smartest thing to do is not to address spirituality at work. First of all, I disagree with that thought. Second, I am not as concerned with the spirituality *at* work as I am the spirituality *of* work.

What does work mean to you? Perhaps there are as many definitions of work as there are of spirituality. For many people, work is a job. It's what they do to pay the bills. They perform the duties expected from their employer in order to make money, not for the sake of the work itself or for creative expression. As a result, the work has no meaning to them. When we see work as a necessary evil, with no meaning other than to earn money to live, we become disengaged. And this is the case even if you enjoy your job.

For others, work is a career. Perhaps they found something they enjoyed doing in a particular job, and it grew into a career. Perhaps they have a set of talents, and they have dedicated their professional life to using those talents in a career. They take pride in the quality of the work they perform and aspire to be recognized and promoted for a job well done. Regardless of how they got there, work for them has evolved into much more than just a single job.

And still for others, work is a calling. They have found the bigger purpose for their existence and understand what they believe their life is all about. They accept their responsibility to make a difference in the world. They have either found a way to do this work and get paid for it, or they do it in addition to their source of income. Either way, their work life is much more than a job.

Only you know what "work" is to you. My goal here is to get you to consider the spirituality of work and what that means to your life. When reports show that most people are dissatisfied in their jobs, I become convinced they haven't made a connection between how they make their money and their purpose in life. As a result, too many people just coast through life without making a meaningful contribution. We must deepen our sense of meaning and purpose.

There are many ways to enhance your spirituality, but I'd like to challenge you to do two things in this *Spirituality* section.

CHALLENGE NINE: FIGURE OUT YOUR BIGGER PURPOSE

Have you identified what your life's work is? Have you found the bigger purpose for your existence and figured out a way to make that your job? If not, don't feel bad. Most people haven't. However, keep in mind the void created by not fulfilling a bigger purpose (whether we're paid for it or not) and how that void contributes to our dissatisfaction in life, which ties to our dissatisfaction in our work. It simply is not possible to start living for the weekday unless we can bounce out of bed every day knowing we're doing something to add value while we're here.

My hope is that you've found your bigger purpose and that it ties directly into your job. If you haven't found your bigger purpose, keep looking. If you have, and it ties directly into your job, congratulations. But if you haven't found your bigger purpose and you're working a job for no other reason than to put food on the table, then your "work" in this world must be what you do outside of your job.

I mentioned that point in a speech a while back, and an audience member came up to the stage after the presentation and said, "I already have a job, and you're telling me in order to be happy I have to go find more work. It just sounds like more work to me."

He was right, it *is* more work. However, it's a different kind of work. When you do work that fulfills a bigger purpose, it should be so fulfilling that it doesn't feel much like work. Only those who have achieved this can understand, and it is my hope you search out your bigger purpose if you haven't made that kind of contribution.

We all have a calling. No, we may not cure cancer or negotiate world peace, but we have a bigger purpose. With that in mind, it is critical not to confuse your job or career (i.e., how you make money) and your work (i.e., your purpose for living).

To get you started, here are some recommended action items to help you figure out your bigger purpose:

❏ *Make time for contemplation.* Many people are busier now than they've ever been. People are raising kids, working a job, taking care of a spouse or parent, and just trying to keep up. If you haven't figured out your bigger purpose, at some point you must make time for contemplation. The chances of you waking up every day and "finding" extra time are slim. Schedule it and commit to keeping your schedule. Use your time in any way you see fit. Meditate if that is your thing. Pray if you choose. Or at least take a moment to pay attention to what is good, positive, and beautiful as you go about your day.

☐ *Depend on a higher power.* A study conducted by the Pew Forum on Religion and Public Life indicated 92 percent of people believe in God or a universal spirit. That's a good start, but I wonder how many of those people depend on that higher power. I appreciate there are some people who will have a different definition for a higher power, and that's okay. I am a Christian, and my higher power is God. But this book is not about trying to get anyone to follow my beliefs about a higher power. If it were, I would have put that on the cover. This book *is* about urging you to weave the many aspects of your life together so you can start living for the week-day as much as for the weekend, and that includes your spirituality. One of the best lessons I've learned in my life is that I can't do it all alone. I must depend on my higher power. My challenges are my own, and I must deal with them. However, I believe my higher power wants me to succeed and is willing to help. Whatever your higher power may be, depend on it. It can't be all about you.

☐ *Define happiness.* Earlier in this book I introduced you to Karen, the woman in the 33 percent of people who are happy in their work environment. One of the questions I asked her was, "Are you happy?" Her response was simple: "What do you mean by *happy*?" Before you can be happy at work you must be happy with you, and before you can figure out your bigger purpose, you need to determine what makes you happy. And by the way, I mean real happiness. Not fishing or hunting. Not playing video games or going to the movies. I'm talking "goose bumps down your spine" kind of happy when you do something that you know makes a difference. Find that kind of happy, and you just may have found your purpose.

CHALLENGE TEN: COMMIT TO A CAUSE GREATER THAN YOURSELF

Day-to-day life can be rather boring. We often look forward to the exciting plans we make because it's an opportunity to do something outside our routine. We get out of bed in the morning, go through our morning rituals, fight the traffic, go to work, deal with our challenges, earn an income to pay the bills, go home, spend time with our family and friends, and then go to bed. We get up the next day and start the process all over again.

Our spiritual development requires us to commit to a cause greater than ourselves. In the fable, the trainer, Dennis, explained the importance of committing to a cause greater than yourself and what that looks like to different people. "Well, it looks different to different people. For one person, it's about becoming a public servant because she doesn't like the way the government takes care of the people. For another, it's dedicating every free moment he has to an organization fighting cancer because he lost his wife to that horrible disease. It's different for everyone. But ultimately, it's about making a commitment to a cause much greater than themselves."

At the end of the fable, we heard from Mattie about the impact it had on her life: "A big part of my spiritual development has been committing to a cause greater than myself. Several things happened when my husband and I committed to helping the Alzheimer's organization. One, we gave ourselves a bigger purpose for our lives than work. Two, we've committed to financially support the organization, so when I wake up and don't want to go to work, I ask myself how I can support our organization if I'm not making the money to do it, and that gives me the motivation to get out of bed and go to work. Three, we've found a purpose for after we retire. We always wondered what we would do in retirement, and this provides the purpose. And four, others around us have seen what we're doing, and it's inspired them to do something similar."

To get you started, here are some recommended action items to help you commit to a cause greater than yourself:

☐ *Find your philanthropic passion.* It's been said that if I want to know what's important to you, all I need to do is take a look at your checkbook. I can figure out your priorities if I can figure out how you spend your money. I suppose the same can be said about how you spend your time.

Once you've determined that committing your-self to a greater cause is important, establish what's important to you and where your passion lies. Figure out what excites you. Figure out what provides the "goose bumps down your spine" feeling when you help fill a need, and you just may have found your philanthropic passion.

☐ *Determine the appropriate organization(s) in your community.* Once you've found your phil-anthropic passion, figure out where you should serve. Unless you live in a very rural area, there will be an organization ready to accept your commitment. If you're passionate about ani-mals, volunteer at an animal shelter. If the thought of someone going to bed hungry makes the hair on the back of your neck stand up, volunteer at a food bank. If you're not sure which organization to help, go online and search for opportunities in your community. There is a fit for your contributions.

☐ *Commit your time, talent, and treasure.* Com-mitting to a cause greater than yourself is about more than writing a check. Organizations need your time, talent, and treasure. Find your orga-nization and donate your time in whatever way it needs. You have been given gifts of talent. My hope is that you use those gifts in your profes-sion. Either way, give your talent away. If you're an attorney, give away some legal advice. If you're an accountant, give away some financial advice. And finally, give of your treasure. Some-one once told me he got more satisfaction from giving his money away than he got from making it. At the time, I thought he was out of his mind. He was right. Only *you* know how much time, talent, and treasure you have. Commit to a cause greater than yourself, and provide your gifts accordingly.

Spiritual development is an individual journey for each person holding this book, and I encourage each of you to figure out your bigger purpose, then commit yourself to a cause greater than yourself.

Conclusion

English author Rose Tremain once wrote, "Life is not a dress rehearsal." As I travel around, I meet people every day who seem to think it is. They don't like their job. They don't like their boss. They drag themselves through an entire week to get to a two-day respite, with no plans other than not being at work.

Many of these people appear as though they're waiting on the side of the stage of life. They seem to be waiting for a better job or a better boss, and if they can't have that, they're waiting for retirement. They're just waiting. Maybe they're waiting for the good part to start. All this waiting is causing them to miss all that life has to offer.

They don't seem to realize they have the ability to control it all by the choices they make. In some

cases, it requires making some really tough decisions, and maybe that's why the side of the stage is
so crowded. Maybe that's why so many people are
waiting for the good part to start. Maybe that's why
so many people are unhappy in life.

You see, we have much more control over
where we are and where we're going in this world
than we think. We choose to accept a job. We
choose to stay in a job we don't like just because
it provides security. We choose not to answer the
hard questions about our career. We choose to
struggle with our finances because we spend our
money instead of getting out of debt. We choose to
struggle with our health because we eat unhealthy
food. We choose to struggle with relationships
because we hang around the wrong people. We
choose to struggle with our spirituality because we
think we can do it all on our own. I could go on and
on about the choices we make in life. But ultimately, where we are today is the result of the
choices we've made in our lives, and where we end
up will be the result of all future choices we make.

Throughout this book you've been given ideas
to help you weave together the five areas of your
life. The impact this book will have on your life will
be the choices you now make. You can choose to
put it on a shelf, or you can create specific actions
to change your behavior. I invested the time to
write this book, and now you've invested the time
to read it. Now it's time to get to work to allow it to
make a difference in your life. Here is my final
challenge to you: *Create a plan within the next 24*

hours based on what you have learned. Pick out those things in each aspect of your life that need some work and begin to weave them together to enhance your life. There is no magic pill. It will require effort on your part. To ensure you don't stop, find an accountability partner. Tell this person what you're doing to improve yourself, and ask that person to hold you accountable. Even better, have that person read this book, and then hold each other accountable.

Someone asked me one time why I had such enthusiasm for my career. There are two reasons: One, I love what I do for a living, and I can't wait to get on a stage to help people lead themselves and those around them. And two, it comes down to simple math. Seven days. There are more days in the workweek than there are on the weekend! That's all the justification I need. Here's to living for the weekday!

ACKNOWLEDGMENTS

Writing a book is an exciting journey. While the writing is enjoyable, the process can be rather lonely at times. A writer starts with an obsession to write something that will impact the reader's life, and this evolves into uncertainty that the words will achieve the desired outcome. While the finished product is the responsibility of the writer, it takes many people to make it all come together. My heart is full of gratitude and appreciation as I think of the many people who have contributed to this book—and to my personal growth and development.

First and foremost, I want to thank my wife, Heather Swindall. Thank you for the love and support you provide as my spouse—and for the insightful suggestions you provided for this book. Thank you for being my business partner, without whom I could not travel the world doing what I do. The countless administrative details you handle make it all possible. Everywhere I go, our clients say, "Heather makes everything so easy!" I echo that comment, and I thank God every day that I get to spend my life with you. I love you with all of my being.

To my mother, Sherron Hartin, thanks for your unwavering loyalty, love, and support for me from my very first day. As I've discussed in this book, much of how we feel about our jobs is tied directly to our home life. Thank you, Mom, for raising me to appreciate the simple things in life.

For me, writing requires peace and quiet, two things most people can't find in the daily surroundings of life. To my friends, Chuck and Sharon Knibbe, thank you for the opportunity to steal away some of that solitude in your cabin at the Knibbe Ranch. The foundation of this book was established while sitting at the kitchen table. And to Jeff and Karen Fox, thanks for your generosity in providing your cabin at the Lonesome Pine Ranch.

To the many people in my life whom I couldn't begin to mention specifically—friends, family, clients, colleagues, mentors, speakers, and fellow authors—thank you for bringing out the best in me and for challenging me to find new ways to make a difference in the lives of those around me.

To the people who made the book possible, starting with my literary attorney John Mason, thanks for your sage advice and guidance through the publishing world. And thanks to the entire team at John Wiley & Sons, Inc., who contributed to putting this book together. In particular, I would like to thank my publisher, Matt Holt, for his support of this project. Thanks to my editor, Shannon Vargo, for your confidence in me as a writer and your tenacity to get this book out. Thanks to Beth Zipko, Kim Dayman, Lauren Freestone, and Christine Furry for your patience and expertise, and to everyone on the marketing, sales, and publicity teams at John Wiley & Sons, Inc.

Most important, I thank God for the many blessings in my life. I simply can't write the words that would express the gratitude I have for Him who created us all in His image. To the Giver of Life goes all the glory.

ABOUT THE AUTHOR

Clint Swindall is the author of *Engaged Leadership: Building a Culture to Overcome Employee Disengagement*. In addition to writing about leadership, he works with Fortune 500 companies, national and state trade associations, government agencies, and nonprofit organizations as a professional speaker, trainer, and consultant.

As the president and CEO of Verbalocity, Inc., a personal development company with a focus on leadership enhancement, Clint travels the world delivering high-content presentations in an entertaining and inspirational style. His clients include American Express, BMW, Hallmark Gold Crown, Valero Energy Corporation, Ingersoll Rand, and Keller Williams Realty.

His success as a professional speaker has led to recognition in the professional speaking industry as a recipient of the Certified Speaking Professional designation. Less than 10 percent of speakers worldwide who belong to the National Speakers Association and the International Federation for Professional Speakers hold this designation.

During time off the road, Clint is busy working in his community. He currently serves on the Board of Directors for GVTC Communications, the largest telephone cooperative in the state of Texas. Along with his wife, he serves on the Board of Directors of the First Chance Foundation, while serving in various leadership positions with their church family at St. Paul Lutheran Church.

Clint lives with his wife Heather in Bulverde, Texas, just north of San Antonio in the Texas Hill Country where they are raising their three girls—Black, Bleu, and Bailey (their three dogs)!